Walk!

The

Alpujarras

with

Charles Davis

DISCOVERY WALKING GUIDES LTD

Walk! The Alpujarras
First Edition - July 2006
Copyright © 2006

Published by
Discovery Walking Guides Ltd
10 Tennyson Close, Northampton NN5 7HJ,
England

Photographs
All photographs in this book were taken by the
author.

Front Cover Photographs

On the Loma de Cáñar route
(Walk 14)

Fuente la Gaseosa, on
Walk 25

The view towards
Trevélez on Walk 27

Cástaras, on Walk 8

ISBN 1-904946-23-2

Text and photographs* © Charles Davis

Walk!
The Alpujarras

CONTENTS

THE WALKS

THE AUTHOR

Charles Davis was born in London, and has lived and worked in the United States, Sudan, Turkey, Ivory Coast, Spain and France. With the onset of middle age, he realised that the urge to roam was better satisfied by walking than bouncing about on the back of a lorry in the middle of the desert, and now divides his time between mountain tops, desk-tops and laptops. He is the author of numerous highly praised and largely unpublished novels (but at the time of writing, this is about to change).

Jeanette Tallegas has spent thirty odd years labouring for the French education system, from which she has finally, gleefully, taken early retirement. Asked what she intends doing now, she resolutely replies, "Nothing". Nonetheless, she does follow the author up various gruelling mountains, frequently alarming younger ramblers who seem to assume that remote and inaccessible places are the preserve of youth.

ACKNOWLEDGEMENTS

My thanks to Jeannette who still, quite unaccountably, sustains an invincible readiness to follow me up remote mountains, and to Ros and David who, only marginally less mysteriously, remain happy to publish the results.

Charles Davis is also the author of:-

34 Alpujarras Walks
ISBN 1-899554-83-1

Walk! La Gomera
(2nd Edition)
ISBN 1-899554-90-4

Walk! Mallorca (North & Mountains)
ISBN 1-899554-92-0

Walk! Mallorca West
ISBN 1-899554-98-X

Walk! La Palma
ISBN 1-904946-06-2

Walk! Axarquía
ISBN 1-904946-08-9

Walk! The Lake District South
ISBN 1-904946-16-X

Walk! Dorset
ISBN 1-904946-20-8

- published by Discovery Walking Guides Ltd.

FOCUS & SCOPE

Situated in the south-east of Spain, the Alpujarras stretch from the high peaks of the **Sierra Nevada** to the shores of the Mediterranean and are defined to the west by the **Lecrín Valley** and to the east by the confluence of the **Andarax** and **Nacimiento** rivers. Resembling in the west the Pyrenees and in the east the high Atlas, they reflect in microcosm the Iberian peninsula's role as a tectonic, botanic, geological, and cultural buffer zone between Europe and Africa. Boasting high peaks, long ridges, deep valleys, idyllic watercourses, lovely woodland, and a host of picturesque villages, they are the setting for some of the best walking in Europe's second most mountainous country.

This book describes walks in the High Alpujarras of **Granada**, traditionally the singular **Alpujarra Alta** or **Nevedense**. Most are low to medium range mountain walks accessible to any averagely fit hill-walker, but there's also a selection of the major summits to the north, including the highest peak on the Spanish mainland, the **Mulhacén**. These high mountain walks call for more preparation and a greater level of fitness, but they're all walks and pose no technical problems. Alternatively, if you just want to potter about and have a picnic, the 'Strolls' are designed to get you out of the car with maximum reward for minimum effort.

WHEN TO GO

Southern Spain is a good walking destination throughout the year, but some general observations may influence when you go to the Alpujarras. Summer is best for the high peaks, though it's worth noting that the temperatures at 3000 metres can still drop to zero during the night, and conditions can change suddenly and dramatically.

At lower altitudes, walking can be hard work in the summer months, though there's generally a refreshing breeze in the evening. The **Tahá de Pitres**, **GRs 7 & 142**, and other low level walks from villages are best enjoyed in spring and late autumn.

In winter anything up to 2000 metres should be accessible, even if you find yourself above the snowline. Weather permitting, the high mountain routes are still feasible, but aren't recommend unless someone in the party is used to winter walking at altitude. Conditions are generally most stable around February.

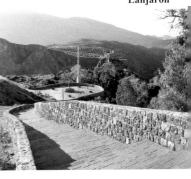

Despite the fun of the festivities, Easter weekend is not a good time to arrive, since every migrant and his dog returns to the *pueblo* to expiate the sins accumulated in the city during the rest of the year, and the weight of traffic ploughing through **Lanjarón** suggests some biblical catastrophe has struck the plains. August is comparably crowded, though you maybe tempted by the village festivals, one of which will have the mountains echoing to the thunder of firecrackers nearly every evening.

GETTING THERE

The cheapest flights are to **Málaga**, though there are charters to **Granada** during the ski season. From **Málaga**, it's best to hire a car at the airport and drive east along the coast to **Salobreña** (E15/N340 direction **Motril/Almería**) then follow the **Valle Lecrín** (N323 direction **Granada**) north to the **Lanjarón** turning (A348) - a 90 minute to 2 hour drive. Otherwise, there's a daily coach to **Órgiva** from the central bus station (dep. 3.30pm, rtn. 8.15am) and a more frequent service changing at **Motril**. Buses between **Málaga** and **Granada** leave on the hour every hour between 7am and 9pm except in the early afternoon when the times are 1.30/2.00/2.30.

Buses from **Granada** to the main Alpujarras villages (except **Cañar**, the lower **Tahá de Pitres**, **Cádiar**, **Cástaras** and **Mecina-Bombarón**) start at 10.30am (terminates at **Pitres**), 12.00am and 5.15pm. **Granada**, **Órgiva**, **Cádiar** and **Mecina-Bombarón** are linked by a service leaving **Granada** at 8.30am and 6pm. Buses from the Alpujarras to **Granada** start from **Alcútar** at 5am and 5pm, from **Pitres** at 3.30pm, and from **Mecina-Bombarón** at 6am and 4.30pm.

GETTING ABOUT

Our network of itineraries should give access to every walker, regardless of budget or means of transport. However, realistically speaking, unless you camp out or are keen on insanely long days, you need a car to climb the higher peaks.

If you don't have a car, you can get from village to village on the GRs (see Walks 1- 9), by the bus service, or taxis (see Appendix C), though the latter are not always to be relied on as it's entirely possible the driver might be busy tending his bar or digging his potatoes. Where relevant (for example, on linear walks), approximate departure times for buses back to the start point are given in the fact summary at the start of each itinerary.

If you're driving, don't forget the *pistas forestales* or forestry tracks (see Appendix A). They can be blocked by snow, landslides or water, but are ideal for exploring further afield. If you come to a stretch you're not sure about, walk a hundred yards or so to get a feel for it. The *pistas forestales* are for driving or riding - I don't recommend walking on them.

THE WALKS

The walks are within the capabilities of anyone who is moderately fit and accustomed to hill-walking. However, don't be overambitious. If you're not used to it, climbing a high mountain can be a deeply unpleasant experience, and coming down even worse. Build up slowly and measure your progress against one of our shorter itineraries then adjust walking times accordingly. Bear in mind that all breaks have been edited out. These are 'pure' walking times and only the super-fit or frankly deranged will complete the walks in the stated time. Allow at least 15 minutes on top of every hour for path-finding, pleasure taking and breath catching.

In the descriptions, I've sought to avoid excessive detail. Nonetheless, tricky points are described minutely and I hope there's enough information to keep you on track and enhance the experience. The number of words does not correspond to distance covered. A paragraph may detail a hundred yards, a line half a mile. It all depends on the complexity of the terrain.

I use the following terms of reference:
- A dirt track is anything a car might use, ranging from well-stabilized *pistas forestales* to sump crunching, suspension mangling surfaces only suited to the most audacious 4WD fanatic.
- Depending on how you look at it, a mule trail is a broad path or a narrow track. Custom held that two mules each with two panniers should be able to pass side by side. Not all mule trails meet this criteria (and it's entirely possible you will meet a mule carrying two bulging panniers), but they are all broader than the average path, usually follow ancient routes between villages, and are often roughly cobbled with rocks.
- A path is a path is a path, except when it's a goat track, which is a wilful sort of 'way' frequently disappearing and splintering into a confusing web calculated to baffle non-herbivorous bipeds. For purposes of consistency, climbs are 'steep', 'steady', or 'gentle'. If you're browsing through the book and find puzzling references to numbered *Pistas Forestales* or PFs, see Appendix A.

WAYMARKED PATHS

Waymarks in Spain tend to be a tad wayward. You can usually rely on the red-and-white GR (*Gran Recorrido*, a Long Distance Path or LDP of 50km or more) stripes, though beware of similar waymarks on forestry tracks indicating old equestrian/4WD routes. In the text, capital GR designates a path, lower-case gr a road administered by the authorities in **Granada**. The yellow-and-white PR (*Pequeño Recorrido* or Short Walk) waymarks vary greatly. On some routes they're dotted about with wanton monotony, on others they're so rare they resemble an endangered species.

The **GR7** is the most famous LDP crossing the region and is described in walks 1-7. It's an excellent introduction to the area and an ideal way of linking the main villages. Treating it as a 'commuting' path, most of our **GR7** itineraries are linear walks. However, not everyone will want to carry their kit about or walk both ways in a day, so I've broken it up to allow for a return to the starting point by bus - except Walk 1, which would involve a bus and a taxi.

The local authorities dub the **GR142** 'Between Peaks & Valleys'; 'Between Tarmac and Kindling' would be an equally valid name, since the pathmakers have displayed an uncanny affinity for asphalt and acres of desiccated scrub just waiting for a brushfire. However, it's not without its attractions, nowhere in the Alpujarras is without its attractions, and the sections covered in our itineraries include some of the prettiest paths in the region.

There are innumerable PRs and short linking paths (SLs or *Senderos Locales*), and more are appearing all the while. Several walks featured in the first edition of this book have since received the official imprimatur of a PR number or incorporate a path subsequently designated an SL, so don't be surprised if more itineraries are dressed up with mapboards and a dab of paint. Bear in mind that our walk may not coincide with the waymarked itinerary.

The most exciting recent development in terms of official paths is a 360 kilometre LDP touring the entire Sierra Nevada, the **Sendero Sulayir**, after the Moorish name for the sierra, *Yabal Sulayr* or 'Mountain of the Sun'. The route should be finished by the time this volume goes to press. For details, see www.sulayr.net.

ACEQUIAS
No visit to the Alpujarras is complete without a walk along one of the *acequias*, irrigation channels tapping the aquifers of the high mountain. Who first developed them is disputed, some crediting the Moors, others the Romans. Either way, it had become a Moorish 'art' by the time Felipe II expelled the remaining Moslems after the rebellion of 1568, as he made one family in each village stay behind to show the Christian settlers how the system worked.

Some *acequias* were hacked into cliff faces by masons suspended over vertiginous drops (beware of following *acequias* without taking a close look at the contour lines on the map), but most follow gentler slopes and are more like ditches, dug into the hillside and reinforced by the skein of roots encouraged by filtration. Occasionally you will see an 'improved' version lined with PVC or concrete to prevent leakage, but probably not for long as the ground tends to dry out, the supporting vegetation dies, the undergrowth rots, and the whole lot falls apart.

Walking along *acequias* is a delight, but remember, these are still working paths. You may see an *acequero* with an adze fishing rocks from the water, clearing obstructions, or rebuilding the wall. For him walking is a chore, not necessarily a pleasure. Recreational walkers should be careful not to exacerbate wear and tear.

FLORA & FAUNA

Details are beyond the scope both of this book and my expertise, but where relevant, likely sightings are mentioned in walk descriptions. The two most emblematic animals, are the mountain goat and the golden eagle. You may also see wild boar (steer clear if they've got a litter of cute little piglets with them), partridge, hoopoe, wasp-catchers, and any number of birds of prey.

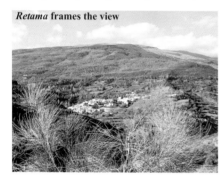

Retama **frames the view**

The most common trees are pine, holm oak, chestnut and ash. I often refer to *retama*, a broom-like shrub from the leguminosae family that's found throughout Southern Spain. If you're not already familiar with it, you'll soon come to recognize its long, splayed fronds speckled with yellow flowers in spring and summer.

Other common or emblematic shrubs and herbs include caper, alyssum, rosemary, thyme, saxifrage, camomile, and more variety of broom than I'd care to name. Insects and flowers are too varied and, sometimes, too unique, to even begin cataloguing. See the Bibliography for relevant publications.

DOGS

Bolstering your ego with something big and slavering does not seem to be an Alpujarran habit. Dogs are friendly or frightened, and frequently noisy. Experience and anecdotal evidence suggest you would be very unlucky indeed to have any unpleasant encounters.

FIRE

In the summer of 2005, a tourist got lost in the woods above **Lanjarón**. Unwilling to spend the night outdoors, the gentlemen in question reckoned it would be a pretty cunning plan if he lit a fire 'to attract attention'. He attracted attention all right. He burned half the mountain down. Enough said. Don't even think about it.

ACCOMMODATION, CAMPING AND REFUGES

Accommodation in the Alpujarras is plentiful and cheap. Except for Christmas, Easter and sometimes August, you should have no trouble finding a room on the spot. For the foreigner, there's a bewildering variety of names advertising accommodation (*pension, hostal, hotel, posada, fonda, camas, habitaciones*), but the distinctions are too fine for consideration.

On the whole, facilities are clean and basic, which is enough for most walkers. If you want something more sophisticated, there are self-catering apartments and *casas rurales* (don't get too excited if you see the latter translated as 'Country Houses'; these are not the sort of places you read about in dentists' waiting-rooms) and some upmarket hotels in the spa town of **Lanjarón**. You could also try the **Hotel Taray** in **Órgiva** or **La Fragua** and the **Alcazaba de Busquístar** in **Trevélez**. See Appendix C for more details and pre-booking options.

Puente Palo (**Pista Forestal 2**, Walks 11-14) is an official camping area without services. There are fully equipped campsites at **Órgiva**, **Pitres** and **Trevélez**.

The only manned refuge in the Alpujarras is the **Poqueira** (tel. 958 343 349, see Walks 21 & 22) above **Capileira**. Some guidebooks and maps still refer to the 'Felix Mendes' despite the fact that it was knocked down several years ago. The following unmanned refuges are on or near the walks described in this book: **Ventura**, **Caballo**, **Cebollar**, **Carihuela**, **Caldera**.

Poqueira refuge

EATING AND DRINKING

The Alpujarran diet is a meat (*carne*) and potatoes affair and generally very good - for the palate if not the arteries! Charcuterie is a specialty and hams hang from every ceiling. Classic local dishes include spiced and/or dried sausages (*chorizo*, *longaniza*, *salchichón*), black pudding (*morcilla*), broad beans fried with ham (*habas con jamón*), and any number of cuts of pork (*cerdo*), lamb (*cordero*), kid (*choto*), rabbit (*conejo*) and chicken (*pollo*), generally griddled (*a la plancha*), smothered in garlic (*ajillo*), or stewed in an earthenware casserole dish (*cazuela*). Beef is elderly veal (*ternera*) and not very exciting. *Lomo* is loin, usually pork, *chuletas* are chops, *bocadillos* are sandwiches, and *casero/a* indicates something home-made.

Doubtless, vegetarians will be disheartened by this carnal catalogue and concluding they'd best bring their vitamin supplements with them ...and rightly so.

As elsewhere in Spain, a 'vegetarian' dish is likely to be a plate of beans with a lump of dripping lard melting all over it, and if you insist on something purely vegetarian, you'll probably get a sorry looking plate of peas and an even sorrier looking waiter. Vegetarian meals are available at **El Jardin** in **Pitres**, **Ibero Fusion** in **Capileira**, and **La Fragua** in **Trevélez**. Otherwise, ask for a *revuelto* (eggs scrambled with vegetables), *tortilla de patatas* (Spanish omelette), *berenjenas fritas* (fried aubergine), *patatas a lo pobre* (potatoes fried with garlic and peppers), or *sopa de ajo* (garlic soup) - and hope the chef has resisted the temptation to embellish it with a little cured ham. *Ensaladas mixtas* are usually 'garnished'

Sun-dried red peppers

with half a tin of tuna.

Despite some trout fishing in local streams, the Alpujarras are not the obvious place for fish (*pescado*), though the ubiquitous salted cod (*bacalao*, as much the national dish as *paella*) is on most menus, and if you can't get to one of the restaurants on the coast, you might like to try *boquerónes* (fresh anchovies), *calamares* (squid rings) or, their babies, *chipirónes*.

The pudding is not an art the Spanish have perfected and often entails a glossy card listing the factory-made ice-creams on offer. However, most places will have rice pudding (*arroz con leche*), cottage cheese with honey (*queso con miel*), crème caramel (*flan*), and an assortment of fresh and dried fruit.

Breakfast (*desayuno*) is equally unimaginative and generally means toasted, baguette-style bread (*tostadas*) with - in descending order of interest - *tomate* (crushed garlic and tomato), *aceite* (olive oil), *mermelada* (jam), or *mantequilla* (butter, which is never as good as the oil).

As for portions, nouvelle cuisine is a concept alien to the Spanish temper and you might wish to order 1 for 2 rather than risk ending up face to face with a steaming pile of pork that would keep a family well-fed for a week. *Tapas* are often still given free with a drink, rather than being a bought appetizer, which they have become in most of Spain. *Raciónes* are larger portions of *tapas*, *platos combinados* a full single-course meal, and the *menú del día* a cheap three-course lunch.

Wine is cheap and generally cheerful. The locals drink *costa* which tastes like a bizarre blend of fortified wine and retsina. Some of it is vile (beware if someone offers you something they are pleased to call 'wine' and claim is 22° proof!), but at its best it goes down with dangerous ease. For good *costa*, try the butcher (*carnicería*) in **Busquístar**.

Alhambra beer (*cerveza*) is not bad by Spanish standards, shorts are never short, *sol y sombra* is a kill-or-cure mixture of brandy and anis often deemed necessary early in the morning (this may explain why the rest of breakfast is so pedestrian), and *carajillo* is the name given to the endearing Spanish habit of brightening up their coffee with a tot of brandy.

Then there's always water; bottled natural or fizzy (*agua sin gas/con gas*) or from *fuentes*. The **Fuente Pedro Calvo** (on the **PFI**) is reputed to have the best water in the Alpujarras.

Fuente Pedro Calvo

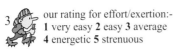 our rating for effort/exertion:-
1 very easy **2** easy **3** average
4 energetic **5** strenuous

 approximate **time** to complete
a walk (compare your times
against ours early in a walk) -
does not include stopping time

 approximate walking
distance in
kilometres

 250m approximate
ascents/descents in
850m metres (N=negligible)

 circular route

 linear route

 figure of eight route

 risk of **vertigo**

 refreshments (may be at start or end of a route only)

- Walk descriptions include:
- timing in minutes, shown as (40M)
- compass directions, shown as (NW)
- heights in metres, shown as (1355m)
- GPS waypoints, shown as (Wp.3)

Notes on the text
Place names are shown in **bold text**, except where we refer to a written sign, when they are enclosed in single quotation marks. Local or unusual words are shown in *italics*, and are explained in the accompanying text.

MAP NOTES

The map sections used in this book have been taken from **Alpujarras Tour & Trail Super-Durable Map** 2nd edition (ISBN 1-904946-25-9) published by Discovery Walking Guides Ltd.

All map sections are aligned so that north is at the top of the page. In the interests of clarity adjoining and inter-linking walking routes have been deleted from the map sections for each specific walking route. Waypoint positions and numbers refer to the walking route illustrated by the map section.

Alpujarras Tour & Trail Super-Durable Map 2nd edition is a 1:40,000 scale full colour map. For more information on DWG publications, write to:-

Discovery Walking Guides Ltd.
10 Tennyson Close
Northampton
NN5 7HJ
England
or visit:
www.walking.demon.co.uk   **www.dwgwalking.co.uk**

THE ALPUJARRAS

Spain

SPAIN

This locator map and the maps accompanying the walk descriptions are adapted from Alpujarras Tour & Trail Super-Durable Map (ISBN 1-904946-25-9) published by Discovery Walking Guides Ltd.

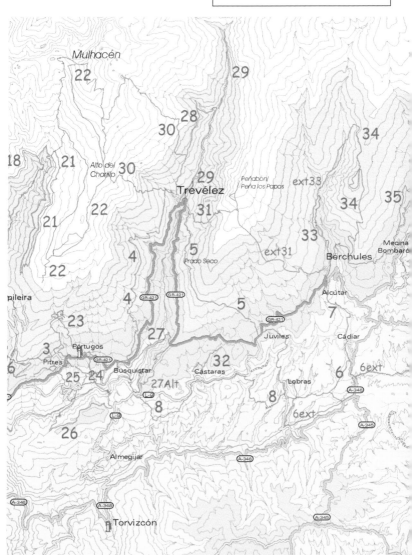

The map sections which accompany the walk descriptions in this book are adapted from:

Alpujarras Tour & Trail Super-Durable Map
(ISBN 1-90494625-9 published by Discovery Walking Guides Ltd.).

This 1:40,000 scale map is recommended for use alongside this book. It is available from bookshops, from amazon.co.uk and direct from the publishers at:

DWG Ltd.
10 Tennyson Close
Northampton NN5 7HJ
England

ALTITUDE, HÖHE, ALTITUD, ALTITUDE

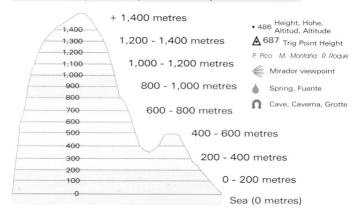

ROADS, STRAßE, CARRETERA, ROUTE

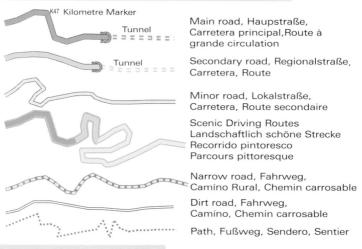

Walking Routes, Wanderweg, Sendero, Chemin.

Walk! The Alpujarras Route (Red)

🚶 17 ⑤ GPS Waypoint
see Waypoint Lists

🏰 Major Hotel 🏠 Important House, Casa Major 🏛 Hotel 🗽 Petrol

🏠 Forestry House, Casa Forestal 🏠 House, Casa 🏚 Ruin/Barn

🗼 Lighthouse, Leuchtturm, Faro, Phare 🍺 Bar/Rest

🗼 Tower, Turm, Torre, Tour 🛈 Information Office 🅿 Parking, Parkplatz

⛪ Church, Kirche, Iglesia, Église ⛪ Chapel, Kapelle, Ermita, Chapelle

🎋 Picnic area, Rastplatz, Zona Recreativa, Pique-nique

⊹ Cemetery, Friedhof, Cementario, Cimetière

⚽ Sports Ground, Sportplatz, Campo deportivo, Terrain de sport

⛺ Camping, Campingplatz, Camping, Camping

🌬 Wind Turbine, Windkraftwerk, Eólica, Éolienne

USING GPS IN THE ALPUJARRAS

The GPS Waypoint lists provided in **Walk! the Alpujarras** are as recorded by the author Charles Davis during his research of the walk descriptions contained in this book. In the interests of clarity, each map section only shows the route and waypoints for that walk. Where a waypoint symbol is shown on a map it has been placed alongside the position to which it refers so as to not obscure the map detail and is numbered so that it can directly identified against the walk description and waypoint list. For readers wondering what we're talking about, GPS Waypoints are also Grid References to the exact locations within each walking route, when used in conjunction with our **Alpujarras Tour & Trail Super-Durable Map** 2nd edition.

The rugged terrain of the Alpujarras region offers the adventurous walker a challenge in every sense of the word. While walking between the villages in the **Poqueira** and **Trevélez** valleys, our Alpujarras PNFs will keep you on the right track or trail among the many navigation choices open to you. Step up in altitude to **El Caballo**, **Mulhacén**, **Siete Lagunas** and our other high altitude routes and you'll find our GPS Tracks and Waypoints a real godsend, as you don't want to waste time and effort hiking the wrong trail, not to mention the danger of being lost in the mountains. If you've doubted the wisdom of buying a modern GPS unit and download lead, here in the Alpujarras you'll get your investment back many-fold.

Most of our routes offer good to excellent GPS reception but close to cliffs your GPS might be confused by reflected signals; not so much a problem as a possibility depending upon the configuration of the satellites. In the small towns and villages it is a different situation where the narrow streets frequently cut off your GPS reception. If you are at the most adventurous end of the walking spectrum you will appreciate that our high altitude routes also have the best 'open sky' GPS reception; a boon on **Pico Alegas** where you can follow Charles' pioneering route through the storm damaged woodlands which is far more difficult without GPS.

In using our Alpujarras PNFs, do take into account the local conditions, geology, tree cover etc. for your expected accuracy of our GPS records. It is virtually impossible to reproduce the exact GPS waypoint co-ordinates in practice when walking a route. While GPS waypoints are quoted to 00.0001 minutes of arc, in practice you should expect 10 metres as an acceptable standard of accuracy when you have '3D navigation' (four or more satellites in view); though good reception in the Alpujarras means that often your accuracy will be closer to 5 metres.

Signal Strength
Signal strength from sufficient satellites is crucial to obtaining an accurate location fix with your GPS unit. In open sky, ridge top, conditions you may have up to 11 satellites in view to give you a GPS location accuracy of 5 metres. Providing you have good batteries, and that you wait until your GPS has full 'satellite acquisition' before starting out, your GPS will perform wonderfully in the Alpujarras for all our routes, subject to the notes above.

To Input the Waypoints
GPS Waypoint co-ordinates are quoted for the WGS84 datum, used to provide grid references on the Tour & Trail Map, in degrees and minutes of Latitude and Longitude. To input the waypoints into your GPS we suggest that you:
● switch on your GPS and select 'simulator' mode,
● check that your GPS is set to the WGS84 datum (its default datum) and the 'location format' 'hddd°.mm.mmm',
● input the GPS Waypoints into a 'Route' file with the same number as the walking route number; then when you call up the 'route' in the Alpujarras there will be no confusion as to which walking route it refers,
● repeat the inputting of routes until you have covered all the routes you plan to walk, or until you have used up the memory capacity of your GPS; you can always re-programme your GPS while in the Alpujarras,
● turn off your GPS. When you turn the GPS back on it should return to its normal navigation mode.

GPS Waypoints are provided as an additional navigation aid to complement the detailed walk descriptions in Walk! the Alpujarras. Knowing exactly where you are in relation to our detailed walk description is a great confidence booster when exploring these new and exciting landscapes. GPS Waypoints are provided for all key navigational points on all walking routes; never again should you find yourself wondering whether you are on the right path or not.

Note that GPS Waypoints complement the detailed walking route descriptions in Walk! the Alpujarras, and are not intended as an alternative to the detailed walking route description.

Personal Navigator Files (PNFs)
Edited versions of all the GPS Tracks and Waypoints compiled during Charles Davis' research are available as PNFs on our **Personal Navigator Files CD version 3.02**. GPS Utility Special edition software is included on the PNFs CD, enabling the user to load GPS Track and Waypoint information direct to their GPS unit via a PC. In addition to the Alpujarras the PNFs CD version 3.02 contains the GPS Tracks and Waypoints for **Mallorca North & Mountains**, **Mallorca West**, **Menorca**, **La Gomera**, **La Palma**, **Tenerife**,

Lanzarote, **Sierra de Aracena**, **Madeira**, **Axarquía**, **Andorr**a, and the full Walk! UK series of guide books covering **Lake District North**, **Lake District South**, **Yorkshire Dales (North & Central)**, **South Pennines**, **Peak District South**, **Brecon Beacons**, **South Downs**, **Dorset**, **Dartmoor** and **Exmoor**.

The PNFs CD version 3.02 is available from Discovery Walking Guides Ltd at £9.99 including postage.

Confused by GPS?
If you are confused by talk of GPS, but are interested in how this modern navigational aid could enhance your walking enjoyment, then simply seek out a copy of **GPS The Easy Way**, the UK's best selling GPS manual. Written in an easy to read, lively, style and lavishly illustrated, GPS The Easy Way takes you through all aspects of GPS usage from absolute basics up to GPS Expert and debunking the myths about GPS along the way, an essential purchase for anyone thinking of buying a GPS. GPS The Easy Way (2nd edition 2006) £4.99 is available from bookshops and post free from:

Discovery Walking Guides Ltd.
10 Tennyson Close
Northampton NN5 7HJ
www.walking.demon.co.uk   www.dwgwalking.co.uk

WALKING EQUIPMENT

Reading the postings on uk.rec.walking internet news group, it is obvious that walkers are very interested in the clothing and equipment used by other walkers. For some this interest borders on obsession, with heated debates over walking poles, boots versus sandals, GPS versus 'map and compass' navigation etc etc. Walking magazines are packed with clothing and equipment reviews, opinions and adverts, but few walking guide books give more than a cursory mention to recommended clothing and equipment. At the risk of upsetting some walking fundamentalists, here is a brief rundown on what we've used during walking research.

Backpack
A 25-30 litre day pack should easily cope with all the equipment you should need for a day's walking. A design with plenty of outside pockets to give easy access to frequently used items, such as ½ litre water bottles, is a good starting point. Well-padded straps will spread the load and a waist strap will stop the pack moving about on the more adventurous routes. A ventilated back panel will help clear sweat on hot days and tough routes; a design with a stand-off frame is best for ventilation and worth the small increase in weight. Do spend time adjusting the straps so that you get the most comfortable fit.

As an alternative to traditional backpack designs, you might find the cyclist's packs produced by Nikko, and similar companies, a good compromise of stand-off frame, capacity, pockets and weight.

Footwear
Never compromise on footwear. While there are many comfortable paths in the region, a lot of the walking is on uneven or unstable surfaces. Whether you

choose boots, shoes or sandals, they must be up to the task. You will need a hard sole with plenty of grip and a well padded foot-bed. One favourite is a pair of Bestard boots that were picked up at their factory shop on Mallorca. Worn with thick mountain socks, these boots have done everything asked of them.

Whichever footwear you choose, do make sure that you have covered plenty of kilometres in them before coming to the Alpujarras.

Sun Protection
Always carry a comfortable sun hat, also useful should it rain. Choose a design that gives you plenty of shade, is comfortable to wear, and stays on your head in windy conditions. You will be spending several hours a day outdoors and sunburnt ears (and neck) are both painful and embarrassing. Sunglasses and high-factor sun cream are highly recommended.

Water & Food
Always carry as much water as you think you might drink. A couple of ½ litre bottles, a few pence each from local shops, is the minimum, and add another couple of litres for more demanding routes. Even on shorter routes, I would advise that you carry some survival rations. While some routes are well equipped with 'tipico' bars these may not be open when you need them, so survival rations of chocolate bars and the like can provide welcome comfort.

Medical Kit
Antiseptic wipes, antiseptic cream, plasters and bandage are supplemented by lip salve, which can seem like a life saver in hot dry conditions. Also include tweezers, which you will soon appreciate if you catch a splinter or cactus spine, and a whistle to attract attention if you get into difficulties.

Navigation
Do not compromise - buy the best guide book and the best map, and carry them with you. A compass is useful to orientate yourself at the start of a route and for general directions, but a GPS unit is far more useful - see 'Using GPS in the Alpujarras' on page 19.

Clothing
Choose loose comfortable clothing and add a lightweight waterproof jacket and extra warm layers to your back pack; depending on when you visit the Alpujarras, you might experience rain, snow, frost, wind and strong sunshine. Be prepared for almost any conditions. See page 8, 'When to Go'.

Other Equipment
You won't want to be carrying excess weight during your walking, especially on the longer routes with major ascents/descents. Digital cameras generally weigh less than their film equivalents, and a monocular is half the weight of a pair of binoculars. Secateurs might seem an unusual choice of walking equipment, but they can be useful on some routes. A mobile phone, and money (refreshments, taxis, public telephones, drinks machines etc.) are also recommended.

The Editors

The route is described in two section, total time for the full route 3 hours 35 minutes.

LANJARÓN- CÁÑAR

This section of the GR7 gives a pleasant introduction to the contrasting landscapes of the Alpujarras, passing through well-irrigated, heavily domesticated land, barren pasture and an attractively wild valley. It's exposed though, so perhaps not ideal in summer.

Views over the Lecrin/Guadalfeo valleys

(one way)

Access:
Park in one of the large lay-bys at the eastern end of **Lanjarón**.

Stroll
From **Cáñar**, follow the GR7 west to Wp.14.

There are no buses back; the nearest taxi is Juan Funes (see Appendix C).

Leaving the car, we follow the **A-348** to a newly restored house (Wp.1), 200 metres east of the **Río Lanjarón** bridge, fifty metres after the **Jamones Artisanos Morillas**. The GR7 starts on the stony path to the left of the house (N.B. NOT the main concrete track, the end of PF1 Branch C, just after the house. Waymarks on this concrete track are for the GR-142, not the GR7).

Behind the house, we take the narrow path climbing away from the GR-142 up to a dirt track behind an old metal water tank, where we bear right and then left onto a minor concrete track up to a modern house with a satellite dish on its fence (Wp.2 5M). We then bear left and immediately turn right onto a wayposted path, which we follow up to a dirt track (Wp.3 10M).

Fifteen metres to the left the path continues climbing, crossing the dirt track again (Wp.4 21M) before rejoining it a few minutes later. We then stay on the track till a dead-end sign (Wp.5 32M) and take the path on the left to follow a wide *acequia* for five minutes to another concrete track.

Turning right, we follow this track till we approach a major junction (PF1 Branch C/GR-142), thirty metres before which old GR markings on a rock to the right indicate a faint path on the left (Wp.6 41M) heading towards the breeze block walls of a goat farm.

Following the path behind the farm brings us back to PF1 (Wp.7 52M) just above a GR-142 signpost, where we cross PF1 onto a branch going east (E) and almost immediately come into sight of **Cáñar**. The track curves (NE) to a junction with another dirt track (Wp.8 60M) on the right to the **Cortijo del Conde** (Walk 9, Wp.8). The GR7 continues on the left (NE) bearing left again at another junction (Wp.9 65M).

The Río Sucio valley

We leave the dirt track a couple of minutes later at two wayposts (Wp.10 67M) to climb (NNE) across abandoned terraces before the path swings right (N) towards pine and fir, after which it descends a slightly precipitous stretch to cross a meagre torrent. For the next thirty minutes, the path dips up and down, winding along a series of goat tracks toward the head of the valley, passing 20 metres below an abandoned *cortijo* (Wp.11 85M) and then crossing a cluster of olive trees, in the middle of which it climbs very slightly to a waypost (Wp.12 89M). It then continues in a northerly direction, (N) winding up and down past oak, pine and fir, and eventually zigzags down to the **Río Sucio** (Wp.13 100M).

On the far side of river, a clearly waymarked path (not nearly so narrow and precipitous as it looks) climbs steeply and curves round the mountain to cross a patch of erosion (Wp.14 120M), just after which **Cáñar** comes back into view, some fifteen minutes away along a clear path crossing an *acequia* (Wp.15 130M) and the road into **Cáñar** (Wp.16) before climbing up to the western side of the church.

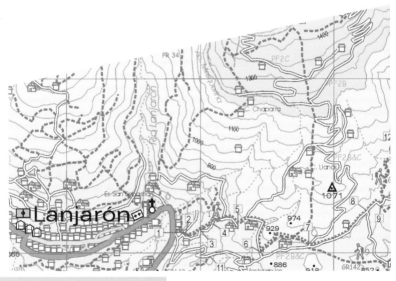

CÁNAR - SOPORTÚJAR

The continuation to **Soportújar** is comparable to the previous section but with better views, easier walking and a perfect rest-stop at the **Río Chico**.

(one way)

| 2 | 1H 20M | 4 km | 50m / ?? | ⟷ | 4 |

Buses at the end of the route :
Soportújar - **Órgiva** (roughly) 4.15/**Órgiva** - **Lanjarón** 5.45

Strolls
(a) From **Cáñar**, follow the GR7 East to **Wp.18**
(b) From **Soportújar**, follow the GR7 West to **Wp.21**
(c) **Soportújar** to **Carataunas** (Wps. 24-25)
(d) **Carataunas** to **Bayacas** (Wps. 25-26)
(e) **Bayacas** to **Órgiva** via the **Río Chico**

Climbing through Cañar

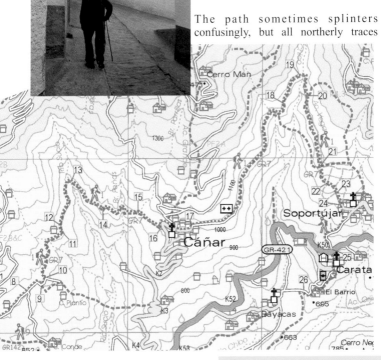

From the *plaza* behind the church, we follow the **Calle Real** (on the left of the **Bar Mesa**) until it bears left next to a green metal door and descends to a concrete track (Wp.17 0M), signposted 'Soportújar'. The track soon dwindles to a path that bears left (N) above the **Río Chico**, passing under shady walnut trees and below the **Cáñar** chestnut forest.

The path sometimes splinters confusingly, but all northerly traces eventually meet. Shortly after a stretch of more varied trees (acacia, poplar, eucalyptus) the path has been destroyed by a landslip (Wp.18 36M). At the time of writing, it has been recently repaired, but be aware that this may be a tricky spot. After the landslip area the path is clear, soon reaching an idyllic glade at the **Río Chico** (Wp.19 45M).

We then cross the river and descend the steps on the far side (SSE) to climb a slightly rough stretch where the path has been washed away and cut by tree-fall. Just after a stone bridge (Wp.20 50M), ignore the narrow path climbing to the left and continue on the main path along the **Acequia de la Vega**, passing one short mildly vertiginous stretch and several ruined huts. (N.B. If you have the alarming sensation that the ground is giving way beneath your feet, don't worry! You're walking on a plastic irrigation pipe and the soil is sometimes thin.)

Ignoring a path climbing across the *acequia* to the left (Wp.21 65M), we take the path below the *acequia*, passing a water-inspection hatch to descend between a stone wall and fields. The path soon bears left (SE), crossing another narrower *acequia* (Wp.22 68M) and continues, descending between fields and bearing left after a small concrete-faced house (Wp.23 74M) to join the concrete track into **Soportújar** (Wp.24 80M) a few minutes later.

If you want to descend to Carataunas
If you want to descend to **Carataunas** (hotel/pension), **Bayacas** (rooms), or **Órgiva** (all services and GR-142), take the **Calle Estación** below the telephone booth beside the church then, just after the **Calle Xanfilla** sign, the **Calle Camino de Carataunas**, which soon turns into a rock-laid mule trail. The path follows a terrace wall to pass between a house and a ruin, after which it dips down, bearing left at a junction before crossing an *acequia* and descending between 'La Rondilla' house and a *Telefónica* hut onto a concrete drive down to the road (Wp.25, 12 minutes from **Soportújar**) 100 metres east of the **Montañero Hotel**, 300 metres east of the **Venta el Venao** (*comidas y camas*). To continue into the centre of the village, cross the road and take the path next to a wooden telegraph pole, which descends directly into **Carataunas** beside the church, fifteen minutes (15M) from **Soportújar**.

For Bayacas or Órgiva
For **Bayacas** or **Órgiva**, continue through **Carataunas** in the same direction and take the concrete lane below the car-park between the **Casa Consistorial** and the telephone booth. After eight minutes (8M), the lane joins a dirt track descending to the semi-abandoned hamlet of **El Barrio**. Follow the path through the hamlet to an *acequia* with a little concrete bridge with *puente* engraved on it (Wp.26 25M from **Soportújar**). For **Bayacas**, continue straight ahead and turn left on the track descending along the **Río Chico** to the bridge into **Bayacas**, thirty minutes (30M) from **Soportújar**.

To continue to **Órgiva**, stay on the left bank till the end of the eucalyptus trees. Cross the *acequia* onto a path below the escarpment that soon comes out on a dirt track above a concrete ford. Follow the track to the BP filling station at **Órgiva**, half-an-hour later.

A slightly irritating start (poor plotting, appalling waymarking), is redeemed by an attractive path passing pretty farm buildings, and is turned into a positive triumph by the food at the **Hostal Guillermo** (though not for vegetarians, I'm afraid). After Wp.2 the path is well marked, though the waymarks are old.

(one way)

Access by car: You can park at the eastern end of **Soportújar** or one hundred metres before Wp.1.

Buses back: 4pm / 6.30pm

Stroll
Park 500 metres up Pista Forestal 2 and follow the GR7 East (Wps. 3-6).

From the *plaza* in front of **Soportújar** church, we follow the road east (E) toward the GR-421 until a wayposted concrete path (Wp.1 5M) leads up to the cemetery.

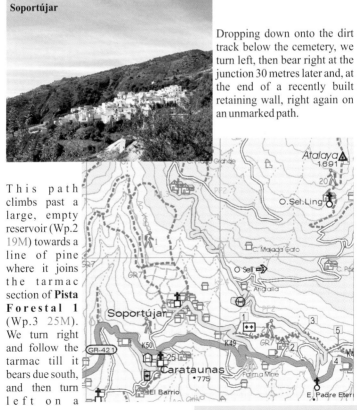

Soportújar

Dropping down onto the dirt track below the cemetery, we turn left, then bear right at the junction 30 metres later and, at the end of a recently built retaining wall, right again on an unmarked path.

This path climbs past a large, empty reservoir (Wp.2 19M) towards a line of pine where it joins the tarmac section of **Pista Forestal 1** (Wp.3 25M). We turn right and follow the tarmac till it bears due south, and then turn left on a

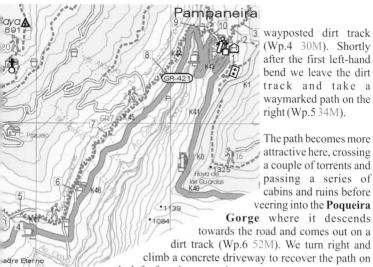

3 wayposted dirt track (Wp.4 30M). Shortly after the first left-hand bend we leave the dirt track and take a waymarked path on the right (Wp.5 34M).

The path becomes more attractive here, crossing a couple of torrents and passing a series of cabins and ruins before veering into the **Poqueira Gorge** where it descends towards the road and comes out on a dirt track (Wp.6 52M). We turn right and climb a concrete driveway to recover the path on the left of two large metal gates.

A few minutes later, the path crosses another torrent and bears right to pass between a large cabin and a high terracing wall. After a few metres of slightly degraded path, we descend along the left branch of two rough *acequias*, then climb between two terraces and cross two more torrents to emerge below a small reservoir (Wp.7 66M) after which the path climbs past more ruins and semi-abandoned huts to the first mulberry trees, announcing the proximity of the village.

The path dips and rises through mulberry, fig and chestnut trees and crosses another narrow torrent, and then passes beneath a long concrete rampart (Wp.8 84M) overlooking **Hostal Guillermo** and the electricity installations of **Pampaneira**. It then gradually descends to the GR-421, which it follows across the bridge (Wp.9 95M) over the **Río de Poqueira**, where we have two options.

For **Pampaneira** village, turn left 100 metres after the bridge onto a narrow path that crosses a dirt track and passes the *Estación Transformadora*, above which a narrow concrete lane (Wp.10 105M) leads into the village. Alternatively, for excellent food (their black pudding is sublime) and a lovely shady terrace, stay on the road another 100 metres for **Hostal Guillermo**.

Pampaneira

Apart from one slightly monotonous stretch (after Wp.5) this is a nice linking path through varied vegetation with several opportunities for making your own itineraries (see the strolls and walks in 15, 17 and Pista Forestal 3). The alternative return route has particularly fine views of the **Tahá** villages and the **Sierras Mecina**, **Contraviessa** and **Lújar**. You can park just in front of Wp.1.

Timing: **Bubíon** - **Pitres** via GR7 (1 hour 20 mins, 4km one way).
Alternative return 1 hour 10 mins (from **Capilerilla**).

Access by car: There is space to park just in front of Wp.1

Strolls
(a) **Capilerilla - Pitres** (Wps. 8-9)
(b) **Capilerilla - Acequia de las Ventajas** (WPs 8-10-6-8)
- also see Pista Forestal 3

Buses back: (from **Pitres**) 3.30pm/6pm, (from **Bubíon**) 2.30pm/7.45pm.

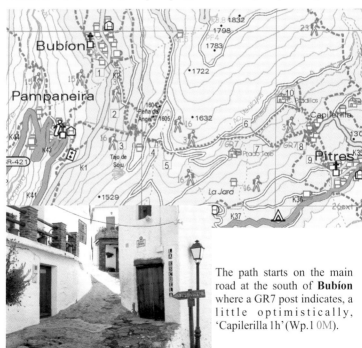

The path starts on the main road at the south of **Bubíon** where a GR7 post indicates, a little optimistically, 'Capilerilla 1h' (Wp.1 0M).

The optimistic sign at Wp.1

We follow the **Calle Ermita** (S), ignoring a path to the left and continuing along a dirt track climbing from lower down in **Bubíon** which soon passes a horse corral with solid wooden gates, then bears left and begins winding uphill.

When the main track bears left (NE) at a water-inspection hatch (Wp.2 13M), we continue straight ahead on the narrower track, and one minute later turn right at a waypost onto a narrow path through oak trees.

This attractive, rocky path climbs steadily past occasional waymarks to a junction of paths (Wp.3 25M) just below an electricity pylon and shortly before the water pipe descending to **Pampaneira** (see Walk 16). We bear left here to climb towards the rocky outcrop of the **Peña del Ángel**. The path goes under the electricity lines and passes a waymarked pylon before descending to a broad dirt track (Wp.4 35M - see PF3 'Tajo de Soju' stroll) near some abandoned transformer towers.

Crossing the main dirt track, we take a minor track (SE) to descend through pine, fir and oak into the **Barranco de la Sangre**, so called for a bloody battle between Christians and Moors, after which the Christians claimed their blood flowed uphill to avoid mingling with that of the Moors!

The graveyard of concrete pipes

Ignoring a track on the right (a potential link to Walk 16's Wp.15), we cross the *barranco*, climbing on the eastern side to a junction of dirt tracks (Wp.5 44M - see Walk 16), just above a 'graveyard' of concrete pipes. We cross the main *pista forestal* and take the track signposted 'Pitres/Capilerilla'.

We then bear right at a Y-junction and right again on a minor track (Wp.6 59M) shortly before a meadow and field of saplings. Just before the chain closing this minor track to traffic, we turn left on a path that descends to join another rough dirt track (Wp.7 65M) which soon dwindles to a path.

Tinaos in Capilerilla

We follow this track/path past a stone signpost for 'Bubíon/Capileira', keeping the old metal fencing posts on our right and ignoring a branch on the right past stone cabins and a large chestnut tree. The path gets rougher as it descends toward a stand of poplars, where it bears left (NE) alongside an ancient retaining wall with pink crosses painted on it, before coming into **Capilerilla** beside a tall poplar and a waypost (Wp.8 75M), 'Bubíon 5.5km/Pitres 0.5'.

A balcony in Capilerilla

Continuing on the path into **Capilerilla**, we pass under a couple of *tinaos* (the terraces that turn streets into tunnels) and, one minute from Wp.8 and immediately after the *ayuntamiento* notice board, turn right onto a concrete lamplit track passing underneath a house, after which it becomes a dirt path leading down to **Pitres** (Wp.9 80M).

Return To Bubíon

To return to **Bubíon**, we take the narrow concrete lane on the left, a few metres east of the *ayuntamiento* noticeboard in **Capilerilla** (0M). The lane climbs under a walnut tree and passes a house on the right, after which it turns into a dirt path climbing NNW, passing a hazelnut tree and a house gated with an old bedstead before bearing right towards a large chestnut tree and a water-hut with a couple of meters mounted on its southern side.

The path then climbs steadily, passing another house and water-hut till it crosses a branch of the **Acequia de las Ventajas** (Wp.10 10M) beside a flimsy waypost for 'Capilerilla'. Ten metres below the *acequia*, on the far side of the tiny meadow with a walnut sapling, there's a nice picnic spot, a grassy platform under shady chestnut trees.

To continue the walk, we turn left at the *acequia* and follow the track leading away from the green metal gates. After passing above the meadow and saplings (chestnut interspersed with vines) seen from Wp.6, ignore the track descending to the left and climb briefly along the main track to rejoin the GR7 at Wp.6, 10 minutes from the *acequia* (20M) and 50 minutes from **Bubíon**.

An attractive woodland route with fine views over the **Trevélez** gorge. Easy to follow and, for the most part, easy walking. Entomologists should head for the **Barranco de la Bina** where there's an incredible variety of insect life. Between the cemetery and Wp.4 the way widens and narrows so often I'll not distinguish between mule-trails and paths, but stick to 'path' for simplicity's sake. Although it's not very steep, the route is riven with *barrancos* that have a certain remorseless quality to them. Every time you think you've finished climbing, you dip down into another *barranco* and scramble up the other side. For the GR7 between **Pitres** and **Busquístar**, see Walk 24. There's plenty of parking on the access road to **Busquístar**.

(N.B. If you're not using our map, beware. On most maps the stretch of the GR7 between Wps. 9 & 11 is dramatically inaccurate.)

(one way)

				500m		
4	4H *	9 km		↗ ↘ 200m	⟷	5

Stroll

* the official timing, 5½ hours, is accurate counting rest-stops

Buses back: 5.30 pm

Bearing left at the cemetery (Wp.1), follow the track till it peters out in a terrace. Drop down onto the next terrace and head east to a low cabin. Take the path down beyond the cabin to rejoin the GR7 (Wp.2) and return to the cemetery.

Busquístar

After crossing the main road opposite the entrance to **Busquístar**, we take the narrow dirt path (Wp.1 0M) climbing past a house/byre to the cemetery. We then bear right and take the concrete track up the eastern side of the cemetery to join a broad path climbing steadily to a major junction (Wp.2 10M), where we bear right again.

One hundred metres later we leave the slightly better trodden goat-tracks and bear left, crossing two terraces and climbing steadily through the oak forest to a rough bridge over the broad **Acequia de Busquístar** (Wp.3 15M).

The path continues climbing steadily before gradually levelling off for an agreeable stroll through the oak forest. After crossing the **Barranco del Tesoro** and its affluents (Wp.4 35M) it climbs to join a dirt track (Wp.5 41M) for a slightly tedious climb round the **Barranco de los Alacranes**. Ignoring branches to the right at 30 metres, 10 metres and 20 metres from Wp.5, we climb steadily through mixed oak and chestnut. Just after the third branch on the right, the track ends among beehives (the **Cristina Mine**). Here we take the narrow wayposted path on the right (Wp.6 62M) and bear right when it joins another path two minutes later.

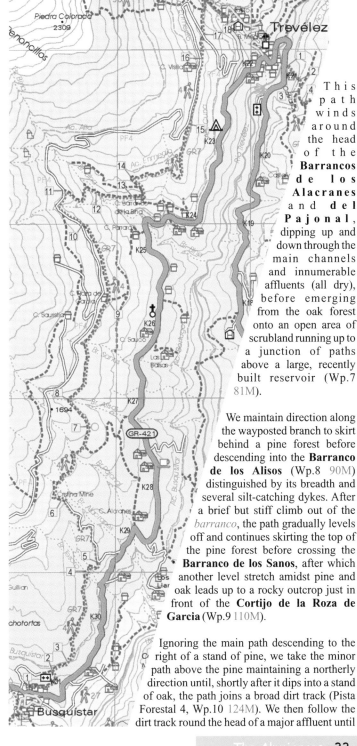

This path winds around the head of the **Barrancos de los Alacranes** and **del Pajonal**, dipping up and down through the main channels and innumerable affluents (all dry), before emerging from the oak forest onto an open area of scrubland running up to a junction of paths above a large, recently built reservoir (Wp.7 81M).

We maintain direction along the wayposted branch to skirt behind a pine forest before descending into the **Barranco de los Alisos** (Wp.8 90M) distinguished by its breadth and several silt-catching dykes. After a brief but stiff climb out of the *barranco*, the path gradually levels off and continues skirting the top of the pine forest before crossing the **Barranco de los Sanos**, after which another level stretch amidst pine and oak leads up to a rocky outcrop just in front of the **Cortijo de la Roza de Garcia** (Wp.9 110M).

Ignoring the main path descending to the right of a stand of pine, we take the minor path above the pine maintaining a northerly direction until, shortly after it dips into a stand of oak, the path joins a broad dirt track (Pista Forestal 4, Wp.10 124M). We then follow the dirt track round the head of a major affluent until the track widens and bears left up towards the head of the **Bina**, where a narrow GR-waymarked path on the right (Wp.11 135M) descends very steeply down the spit of land dividing the affluent from the main *barranco*. The path zigzags down through pine and oak before bearing left to cross an *acequia* for a final steep descent to the welcome oasis of the **Bina** (Wp.12 150M) the only *barranco* on this route likely to have any water in it.

The path out of the *barranco* climbs steeply (E) along the left bank of the **Bina** (thankfully not so steeply as on the right bank) to a rough wire and wood gate. We bear right shortly after this gate for a gentle descent to another gate, after which the path winds along the hillside to pass behind a white-painted ruin with deeply fissured walls (**Cortijo Barranco de la Bina** Wp.13 165M), where it resumes climbing steeply, passing a series of wayposts and occasional waymarks and cairns, before bearing left towards the head of the *barranco*.

We take the third turning on the right (Wp.14 179M, marked by three wayposts) into the pine wood and, after a brief level section, resume the inevitable criss-crossing of subsidiary *barrancos*, fortunately much shallower here. After the fourth dry watercourse, we ignore a branch on the right and follow the main traces on the left, emerging from the pine 150 metres later to climb along an exposed ridge.

Trevélez

Ignoring a minor branch to the left, we cross a barbed-wire fence/gate to climb gently through scattered rocks and pine, passing below a ruined *cortijo*, after which we see **Trevélez** clearly. Maintaining direction, we then wind round the mountainside to eventually rejoin Pista Forestal 4 (Wp.15 203M).

(N.B. If you're coming from **Trevélez**, this turning is not well indicated. It comes 600 metres after you join the Pista Forestal near a grassy platform with a waypost and an apple tree. The clear narrow path is on the left, a few metres before a line of pine and is marked on your right by a small 'GR' cross on a rock in the embankment.)

For **Trevélez**, we follow the dirt track north (N) for 600 metres and then bear right onto a narrow blackberry-lined path (Wp.16 214M) which descends to recross the dirt track lower down (Wp.17 220M). We continue along this path, crossing the **Río Chico** and following the left bank of the river into **Trevélez' Barrio Alto** at the end of **Calle Charquillo** (Wp.18 225M), a considerably more attractive arrival in the town than that endured by those hapless souls dragging round the mountains in their cars and coaches, fetching up in the dreary tourist strip down by the river. Sadly though, that's where we've got to go if we want to catch the bus back to **Busquístar**!

(N.B. If you're doing this route in reverse, ignore a branch on the right between the **Río Chico** and Wp.17. This is Wp.14 of Walk 30, the way up to the **Mirador de Trevélez**.)

This section of the GR7 starts with an easy climb through pine and craggy rocks with an agreeably 'high-mountain' feel. The descent to **Juviles** is more exposed and might be a bit hot in the height of summer. The route can easily be done in reverse, since the waymarks out of **Juviles** appear to have been made with an east-west trajectory in mind. Park next to the bridge at the bottom of **Trevélez**.

(one way)

Trevélez

2	2H 10M	7 km	300m / 200m	3

Buses back: (from **Juviles**) 5.15pm, (from **Trevélez**) 3.15pm/8.30pm

Strolls
(a) From **Trevélez** Wps. 1-3
(b) From **Juviles** climb to Wp.11 then bear right and follow the dirt track back down to the east of the village.

The start of the route (Wp.1)

Eighty metres after the **Río Trevélez** bridge, we take the wayposted path 'Juviles, 3h' (Wp.1 0M), climbing SE. Ignoring a branch on the left in front of a small spring, we bear right to cross the remains of an abandoned *acequia*.

After climbing steadily and passing two houses, we cross a second *acequia*, the **Acequia de Cástaras** (Wp.2 10M) and bear right, ignoring all branch paths, notably the way up to **Peñabón** (an alternative route to the villages of the Eastern Alpujarras, see Walk 31). The GR7 descends slightly to cross the **Calvario** gully then climbs to a small concrete hut (Wp.3 26M) opposite **Trevélez** campsite.

We take the higher of two paths heading south (S) from the hut to join a slightly confused and poorly marked section into the **Barranco de los Castaños**. Maintaining level and direction, we aim for the large threshing circle behind the **Cortijo de los Castaños**, 100 metres before which the path crosses a grassy area fringed with chestnuts (Wp.4 37M) before bearing left just above the chestnuts.

Skirting the southern side of the grassy slope, we head toward an ash at the top of the wood. We then bear right (S) at the ash, staying above the wood, before descending onto a lower terrace and a clearer path running up to a ford across the **Castaños** torrent, where there are two unmarked paths.

Ignoring the broader path on the right, we take the narrower path climbing steeply away from the torrent.

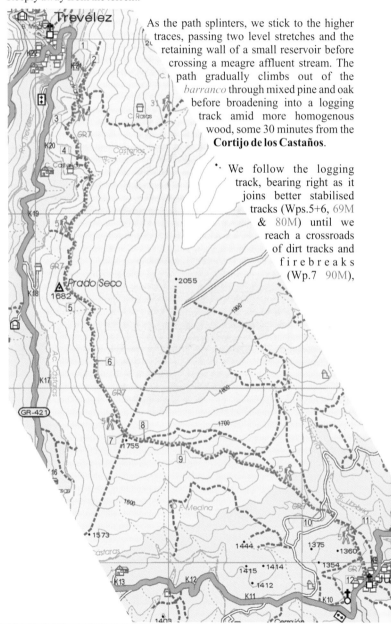

As the path splinters, we stick to the higher traces, passing two level stretches and the retaining wall of a small reservoir before crossing a meagre affluent stream. The path gradually climbs out of the *barranco* through mixed pine and oak before broadening into a logging track amid more homogenous wood, some 30 minutes from the **Cortijo de los Castaños**.

We follow the logging track, bearing right as it joins better stabilised tracks (Wps.5+6, 69M & 80M) until we reach a crossroads of dirt tracks and firebreaks (Wp.7 90M), where the route becomes more exposed, crossing a scrubland of broom, thyme, gorse and alyssum.

We continue straight ahead on a rough track between wire fences and, at the end of the fencing, bear right onto a narrow wayposted path across the scrub (Wp.8 92M) crossing a succession of gullies and small ravines.

Immediately after the second slightly deeper gully, a waypost indicates that the GR7 leaves the main traces and bears right (Wp.9 101M) before resuming a SE direction towards **Juviles**, the southernmost houses of which are now visible. The same bearings hold after crossing another gully, this one distinguished by a small grassy patch with an eglantine bush in the middle: bear right alongside the gully, then left towards **Juviles**.

After crossing several minor gullies, the path leads onto a spur from where **Juviles** is clearly visible - happily, as the waymarks have all been painted for people coming in the opposite direction.

The path broadens as it descends this spur before bearing left to cross a dirt track (Wp.10 115M), beyond which we can either follow a minor branch track or take the poorly wayposted shortcuts down to a couple of white water-huts above a reservoir. Passing to the left of the reservoir, we cross a broad bare slope to twin waymarked holm oaks, below which there is a rough dirt track (Wp.11 125M).

We turn right and, 10 metres later, leave the dirt track to take a narrow unmarked path between fields and orchards, joining a broad concrete lane next to a waterhut which leads into the centre of **Juviles** (Wp.12 130M).

... joining a broad concrete lane ...

An attractive, low mountain walk of contrasts, linking some wild, secluded spots with areas of thoroughly domesticated landscape, and several of the Alpujarras' less celebrated settlements. **Tímar** and **Lobras** in particular are sleepy little hamlets that seem wholly unaware of the tourists trundling through the more famous villages to the north. I don't recommend this route in the height of summer, but it's ideal for winter, or spring and autumn evenings. The extension makes a short loop between **Lobras** and **Cádiar** via the GR142. There's also a link with the GR142 back to **Busquístar** for longer circuits (see Walk 8). There's plenty of parking along the main road through **Juviles**.

For the full route, including the loop:

Juviles-Cádiar: 2 hours 40 mins, 8 kilometres (one-way)
Cádiar-Lobras: 1 hour 50 mins, 7 kilometres (one-way)
Lobras-Cádiar loop: 3 hours, 10 kilometres

N.B.
Beware of the official waypost times; if they are to be believed, the **Juviles-Tímar** stretch takes 45 minutes downhill and 40 minutes uphill, the GR142 between **Cádiar** and **Lobras** makes no progress whatsoever in the course of twenty minutes' walking, while a 100 metre stroll past the chemist in **Lobras** sets you back half-an-hour!

Buses back: don't exist; however there is a bus from **Cádiar** to **Órgiva** (5pm) where you could pick up the 6.45pm bus to **Juviles**; alternatively, if you're feeling energetic, in a little over an hour you can climb to **Alcútar** (see Walk 7) for the 5pm bus to **Juviles**.

From the eastern limit of **Juviles**, next to the Jamones de Juviles building (Wp.1 0M), we take the **Calle Escuela** and bear left after 50 metres onto a wayposted dirt track.

Strolls
(a) **Juviles** - **El Fuerte** (turn right at Wp.2)
(b) **Juviles** - **Tímar** (Wps. 1-4)
(c) **Tímar** - **Lobras** (Wps. 5-8) returning via the road
(d) **Lobras** - **Junta de los Barrancos** via the GRs (Wps. 9/10/25/26)
(e) **Cádiar**-**Río Guadalfeo** (Wps. 16-13)
(f) **Rambla Vereda**: from the A-348 take the **Lobras** road down to the **Río Guadalfeo** and park at the bridge. Stroll along the *barranco* to the junction of the GRs (Wps. 24 & 10).
(g) Heading east off the map, the GR142 **Venta de Cuatro Caminos** to **Cortijo Fuente La Virgen**. From the new bridge at the southern end of **Cádiar** (Wp.15), take the slip road 300m up to turn right on the A348 by-pass, setting the odometer at 0 at the junction with the main road. At 700m, turn left on a dirt track to join the GR142 (Wp.16 EXT*/**Cuatro Caminos**) on a loop of the old road. Follow the dirt track, the **Rambla de Retenil**, to the **Fuente de la Virgen** *cortijo* at the end of the dramatic cliffs just past an abandoned factory. N.B. This route can also be done by car in dry conditions. The GR142 continues (off our map) to **Jorairátar**.

We then follow the dirt track across the **Barranco de Umbría**, ignoring a branch on the left as we climb towards **El Fuerte**, the rocky outcrop separating **Juviles** from **Tímar**.

The track dwindles to a path that crosses an *acequia* shortly before a junction (Wp.2 14M). The branch on the right climbs **El Fuerte**, but we bear left, staying on the GR7 down to the dramatic pass at the head of the **Barranco de Lobras** between **El Fuerte** and the **Alto del Calar**, where there's another waypost (Wp.3 25M) and a clear rocky path down to the north-eastern tip of **Tímar** (Wp.4 35M).

The clear rocky path after Wp.3

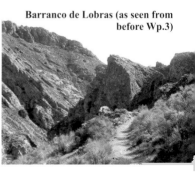

The threshing circle at Wp.5

After descending to **Tímar** church, we bear right along the concrete lane fronting the village, then follow the new **Nieles** road down past the cemetery to a threshing circle pebbled like a sundial (Wp.5 45M) where we bear left (S) on a mule trail through orchards and olive groves.

Ignoring two cobbled branches to the left, we stay on the main trail till it leaves the cultivated terraces to cross scrubland and a rough firebreak before descending to a badly eroded col with a dirt track running in from the right (NW, Wp.6 55M).

We turn left here on a clear path down into the **Barranco de Lobras**. On the far side of the *barranco*, the path climbs SSE, gently at first then more steeply, before levelling out alongside a concrete *acequia* (Wp.7 70M). We bear right along the *acequia* path until a junction of dirt tracks (Wp.8 72M) where we turn left on the main track and, after 50 metres, join the road just north of **Lobras** (Wayposted 'Tímar 40 mins').

Barranco de Lobras (as seen from before Wp.3)

For refreshment, there's a pokey but pleasing little bar off the square behind the church, otherwise we stay on the main road past the village (S), passing the GR142 (E) to **Cádiar** (on the left after the *fuente*). We then 'lose' 30 minutes (watch the wayposts) and pass the GR142 (W) to **Busquístar**, soon after which we turn left on a narrow path between a parking area and a building with red doors and a vine arbour (Wp.9 89M).

The narrow path leads to an almond grove and a mule trail winding down between olive groves to the junction of the **Barrancos de Escalona** & **Atalaya** where the GRs 7 & 142 intersect again (Wp.10 100M).

Beyond the GR junction, we cross the *rambla* into an abandoned olive grove where a broad goat track climbs steeply on the right. Ignoring the goat track, we bear left, heading for a clearly waymarked stump, beyond which a waypost marks the start of a path that climbs less abruptly.

The GR7 follows this well-marked path as it winds up a *retama* covered hillside to a fig orchard (N.B. windfalls have seeded themselves along the path and give great fruit in early autumn, unlike most wild figs which normally dry and rot without ripening) where it crosses a dirt track (Wp.11 110M) before continuing through scrub and levelling out above the tree-lined **Río Guadalfeo**.

After winding round the head of a small gully, a gradual descent leads to an *acequia* where, after a very brief climb towards a scattering of olive trees, we bear right at a junction (Wp.12 120M) to cross the *acequia*. We then follow the *acequia* till the path dips down at a fine blackberry bush (another reason for doing this route in autumn), after which it recrosses the *acequia* and runs along a carefully built retaining wall to pass a ruin and an unmarked junction of dirt tracks (Wp.13 125M).

We carry straight on, passing another junction a couple of minutes later with a signposted path on the right – 'Alqueria de Moraya Hotel/Restaurant 500m' (see Appendix C).

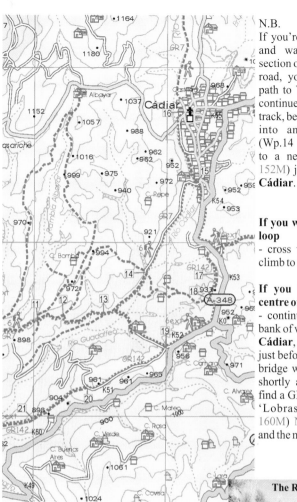

N.B.
If you're doing the circuit and want to avoid the section of the GR142 on the road, you could take this path to Wp.19. Otherwise, continue on the main dirt track, bearing left as it feeds into another dirt track (Wp.14 136M) which leads to a new bridge (Wp.15 152M) just to the south of **Cádiar**.

If you want to do the full loop
- cross the river here and climb to the main road.

If you want to go into centre of Cádiar
- continue along the right bank of what is now the **Río Cádiar**, crossing the river just before a small concrete bridge with green railings, shortly after which you'll find a GR7 signpost saying 'Lobras 1h45' (Wp.16 160M) NW of the church and the municipal market.

The Río Cádiar

EXTENSION
For the GR142 from **Cádiar** to **Lobras**, from Wp.15 we follow the **Venta de Cuatro Caminos** stroll (g) (on foot, alas, and without the odometer - see above) to (Wp.16 EXT*), then head west rather than east, following the *rambla* through the tunnel under the road and, 100 metres later, bearing left to climb over a rise to a wayposted dirt track (Wp.17, ten minutes from Wp.15). After bearing left then left again at an unmarked junction (Wp.18 15M), we rejoin the A-348 (this is the GR142 after all!).

We then follow the road to the junction with the A-345 and turn right to continue along the A-348 to the driveway of the **Alqueria de Moraya Hotel** (Wp.19 24M).

From the driveway, we take the dirt track climbing the ridge on the left for fine views of the **Sierra Nevada**. Ignoring a branch on the left, we follow the dirt track till it bears right. We leave the dirt track next to a waypost and two waymarked trees (Wp.20 39M) and descend to the left of an old reservoir alongside a newly planted vineyard. The path may be ploughed up after the reservoir, in which case we maintain a south-west to westerly direction toward a small ruin, just before which there are a couple of wayposts.

Leaving the ruin on our right, we take a rough dirt track across an almond grove, crossing another track (Wp.21 50M) to continue (SWW) through a field of almonds and figs. When the dirt track along the ridge eventually peters out, we bear right and follow a firebreak until it dips down to a small col (Wp.22 61M).

Taking the broad path on the right, we descend rapidly to rejoin the firebreak, which we follow down a steep slope to a ruined mill at the junction of the **Río Guadalfeo** and the **Barranco del Lagarto** (Wp.23 65M).

Rambla Vereda

We then cross the **Guadalfeo** and, 100 metres after the bridge, bear right (Wp.24 70M) into the **Rambla Vereda** running up to the **Barrancos de Escalona** & **Atalaya**.

After 10 minutes a GR-sign 'Lobras 1h' seems to send us up a hill on the right, but in fact the itinerary continues along the riverbed for an attractively wild stroll to the junction of the GRs (Wp.10) 20 minutes from the road.

The GR142 climbs the spur to the north between the two *barrancos*, though you wouldn't know it from the waymarks. Ignoring the clearer goat tracks to the left of the ridge, we bear right from the tip of the spur and scramble straight up the ridge for a steep climb to a waymarked concrete electricity pylon.

Behind the pylon, a firebreak runs up to a waypost (Wp.25 98M) where the GR leaves the firebreak and bears left to cross two gullies before climbing to a threshing circle next to an acacia tree. Bearing right (N) away from the threshing circle, we skirt the head of another gully and follow the goat tracks into **Lobras** (Wp.26 120M).

A 'commuting path' linking the three villages at the eastern limit of our map. The landscape is relatively domestic, but no less interesting for that, and the villages are just as attractive as the better known ones to the west, perhaps even more so since they are free of the more garish symptoms of tourism. **Bérchules**, in particular, is an unjustly neglected village with full services and some great walks.

Bérchules

There are plenty of bars and restaurants en route and, with an early start, this walk could lead to a leisurely lunch in **Mecina-Bombarón** before taking the afternoon bus back to **Cádiar**.

Buses back: 4.30pm

Parking in the **Plaza de la Iglesia** in **Cádiar** (Wp.1 0M), we take the street behind the *Mercado Municipal*, then the concrete lane down to the **Río Cádiar**. Bearing right at the GR7 waypost ('Lobras 1h45'/Walk 6), we follow the partially concreted track between orchards and houses. When the track turns left toward the river (Wp.2 11M), we bear right along a path between fields, rejoining the dirt track 5 minutes later. The track soon runs into the dry riverbed where it dwindles to a path.

Strolls
(a) **Cádiar - Narila** (Wps. 1-3)
(b) **Bérchules Camino al Río** (Wps. 8-9). Bear right just before Wp.9 for a fine bathing pool 100 metres down river (but beware of slippery rocks).

(For **Golco** strolls, see the end of the main walk description)

After climbing back onto the embankment to bypass a large pipe across the river, the traces become rather confused. Ignoring the apparently clearer route on the right bank beside the poplars, we stay on or near the left bank until we're level with **Narila** church-tower, where a clear but confusingly waymarked path leads away from the river to cross a small *acequia* and climb into **Narila** just below a well-maintained house with a millstone propped beside its front door (Wp.3 24M).

To cross **Narila**, we take the first concreted lane on the left, then first left again. We then follow this street until it bears right past a walled garden with a fig tree at one end and a walnut at the other, then turn left at the T-junction and follow the concrete lane to the northern end of the village, where a GR7 waypost beside a large water hut indicates 'Alcútar 1h' (Wp.4 30M).

We follow the concrete lane back down to the river, ignoring a track and a path climbing to the right and, shortly after the concrete gives way to dirt, a branch on the left into the riverbed. Staying on the main dirt track for a gentle climb past a stand of poplars, we bear left (just before another concreted section) on a rough dirt track across the river, where another narrow dirt track climbs to a Y-junction. Bearing right at the Y-junction, we follow the dirt track for an increasingly steep climb to a terrace, where the GR7 turns right onto a broad path (Wp.5 45M) that soon turns into a rock-laid mule trail. We then follow the mule trail as it winds up between the terraces to cross another dirt track (Wp.6 56M) before coming into the lower part of **Alcútar** behind a large farm building (Wp.7 72M).

Bearing left on a partially concreted lane, we climb steeply into the village to pass a GR7 waypost, 'Narila 40''. We then turn right at the junction just after the waypost and follow the alley as it bears left after House No. 6, then right along the **Calle Cantera** into the **Plaza de la Iglesia**. Beyond this *plaza* are the supermarket and the main road (GR421) which we take, at some peril to life and limb, up to **Bérchules**.

The miraculous *fuente*

Following the road into **Bérchules**, we pass a miraculous *fuente* which might come in handy if you're feeling lonely, since one drink of its waters is supposed to guarantee the instant attainment of an ideal spouse. Spouse or no, our itinerary then takes the **Calle Iglesia** past the church, crosses the **Plaza Abastos**, and follows the **Calle Real** before bearing right on the **Calle Agua**, at the end of which (Wp.8 93M) you'll find the **Camino al Río** and the GR7 waypost, 'Mecina-Bombarón 2h'.

The old GR waypost was on its last legs when we returned to revise this walk. The new metal sign is altogether more sturdy and altogether more confusing, giving the impression that the GR goes up. It doesn't - down's the way.

The path descends rapidly, crossing a litter strewn watercourse, after which it levels out for a couple of minutes before starting its final descent from a threshing circle down to the bridge over the **Río Grande** (Wp.9 110M). On the far side of the river, a rock-laid path (where one can occasionally see *cabra montés*) zigzags up a gully before bearing right on a dirt stretch leading to an old stone wall.

We climb alongside this wall and, when it ends, continue climbing (SE) until the path broadens briefly before running into a junction (Wp.10 134M). Taking the waypost ed branch on the right, we pass a few almond trees before bearing right towards a small stone byre. Passing in front of the byre, we follow a stone terracing wall, after which a gentle climb along a clear path (S) leads to a dirt track (Wp.11 145M).

We bear right here for a brief climb before the track levels off and joins another larger dirt track (Wp.12 155M/**PF5**) which we follow (E) all the way to **Mecina-Bombarón**. Shortly after a concreted stretch through pine trees,

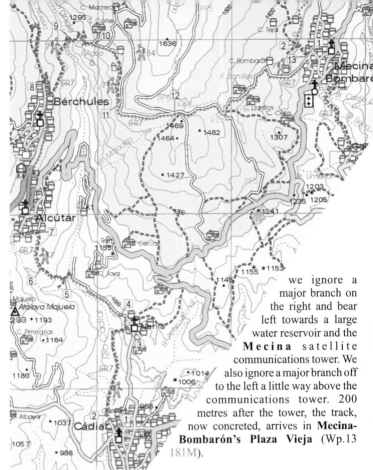

we ignore a major branch on the right and bear left towards a large water reservoir and the **Mecina** satellite communications tower. We also ignore a major branch off to the left a little way above the communications tower. 200 metres after the tower, the track, now concreted, arrives in **Mecina-Bombarón's Plaza Vieja** (Wp.13 181M).

The section of the GR7 covered by our map does not actually end here and you may wish to extend your walk to **Golco** or try one of the following strolls (N.B. the bus does not stop at **Golco**):

Mecina-Bombarón - Golco
From the central square on the main road through **Mecina-Bombarón**, take the **Calle Iglesia Vieja** below the GR7 waypost, 'Golco 20''. Bear right after a second waypost onto a concreted lane which runs into two dirt paths. Take the broad path on the right to arrive in **Golco** a few metres above the **Golco Camino al Río**.

Golco Camino al Río
30 metres behind the church, take the concrete lane down past the lower part of the village, passing a little picnic spot, where the concrete turns to dirt. Shortly after a second narrow concreted section, just as the track bears right, turn left onto a narrow path down to a large threshing circle, after which a rough path descends to a another narrow dirt track. Bear left then right at the Y-junction, where the track dwindles to a path descending to the river and a pleasant picnic spot, beyond which the GR7 continues to **Montenegro** and **Yegen**.

Dipping up and down like a roller coaster, this stretch of the GR142 can seem quite gruelling, but though it boasts some classic GR142 qualities (see Introduction), it also appeals to more conventional ramblers' criteria. The mule trails adjacent to **Notáez** are as nice as any in the **Tahá**, **Cástaras** is a lovely little oasis of green, and the route also provides a useful link between sections of the GR7. If you haven't yet done any walks in the **Tahá**, this will also be your first introduction to the remarkable passes through the **Sierra Mecina (Wp.11+)** that were so vital to the Moorish silk trade. It's a relatively complicated itinerary, but surprisingly well waymarked, and nobody has, as yet, concluded it would be a witty idea to uproot the wayposts. Best in the cooler seasons, but pleasant in the summer if you start early in the morning or late in the afternoon. It could easily be done in the opposite direction, taking the 'Camino del Río' from **Busquístar** then following the GR waymarks.

4/5*   4H   11 km   600m / 400m   5 **

* 5 in summer, 4 at any other time   ** in **Cástaras**

Buses back: no direct buses, though if you set off early, you could catch the 2.55pm to **Juviles** and follow Walk 6 back to **Lobras**. Beware of doing it both ways on a summer's day; I did and it was not a good idea.

Strolls

(a) From the junction of the **Trevélez/Cástaras** roads (Wp.11), take the GR142 until the steep descent begins at the rock-laid section.

(b) Start of **Notáez – Cástaras** (Wps. 9-8)

(c) Start of **Cástaras – Notáez** (Wps. 6-7); bear left when the mule trail crosses the cemetery track which we follow onto the promontory.

(d) **Busquístar, Camino al Río**. From the main square in **Busquístar**, take the concrete lane to the right of **Bar Vargas**. Bear right, away from the 'Camino Helechal' (Walk 27), then take the second left and follow the concrete lane down to the **Camino al Río** sign (Wp.13) and the path down to the river. Just before the bridge (Wp.12), a path on the left goes upriver past several plunge-pools to the old electricity installations.

To reach the start, we take the concrete alley out of **Lobras** church square, to the right of the *correos* office. We then bear left at the Y-junction just beyond a small *fuente* and follow the main road down to a GR signpost, 'Cádiar 1h45 / Nieles 1h30' (Wp.1 0M).

Here we bear right on the concrete (later dirt) track down to the **Barranco de Lobras**, beyond which the track winds up the **Lobrasan** rise and bears left above the **Barranco de la Cabaña**. 100 metres after a couple of electricity pylons (one metal, one concrete), we leave the dirt track (Wp.2 33M) and turn right to skirt an almond grove with a large waymarked olive tree on our left.

At the top of the almond grove, we bear left onto a rough farm track climbing past a breeze-block hut, after which it becomes increasingly overgrown. 100 metres after a shallow cutting and two large *acequia* taps, the track bears right in sight of **Nieles** and we take the narrow path on the left (Wp.3 44M) gradually descending into the **Rambla de Nieles**.

The road to Cástaras

After crossing the shallow stream (Wp.4 54M) at the bottom of the valley, we climb a rough path on the other side that soon runs into an ancient mule trail. The trail crosses an eroded stretch after about ten minutes and enters **Nieles** above a *lavadero* (Wp5 69M), where we turn left onto the road signposted for **Cástaras**.

The road climbs to pass under an aqueduct from where you can see the tip of **Cástaras** perched on the cliffs overlooking the **Rambla de Cástaras**. Glance left and right, and you will appreciate why the GR follows the road here, all options involving a very rough climb or a very rough descent.

Cástaras

Entering **Cástaras**, we go to the right of the church (Wp.6 99M) passing (on our right, and definitely worth visiting) the last bar before **Busquístar**. We then take the street in front of the church doors up to a four-spouted fountain and the **Bar/Pension Maria** (usually closed, but apparently you only have to knock to find a bed for the night).

The alley on the right immediately beyond the bar leads us to a waymarked stone pillar, from where a concrete track descends to an *acequia*, the gated entrance to a house and, on the right, the GR142 path. This path crosses the **Barrancos de Fuente Medina** and **Alberquilla** to join a mule trail leading towards the cemetery. When the main trail bears left in a SE direction toward the cemetery, we take the rougher trail (Wp.7 115M) climbing to the right. We then cross the new dirt track to the cemetery and follow the path as it climbs towards the **Cástaras-Torviscón** road.

The path levels out for 10-15 minutes, passing between almond groves till it gradually descends and actually runs into an almond grove at a point marked by three wayposts (Wp.8 136M). Bearing right, we cross the middle of the almond grove, coming into sight of **Notáez** about halfway across. Toward the edge of the almond grove, the GR bears left past a couple of waymarked trees, at the second of which it turns sharp left onto a narrow path zigzagging down the slope to come out behind the rocky spine to the SW.

Ignoring the tractor tracks that descend all the way to the spine, we follow the narrow path as it bears right, away from the spine, towards **Notáez**. After crossing a small dry *barranco* and descending through yet another almond grove, the path follows the contour lines to join a partially rock-laid mule trail.

After a broad, sandy stretch, the mule trail makes a final zigzagging descent to cross a bridge over one of the affluents of the **Rambla de Notáez**, then climbs into the village beside two GR waypods (Wp.9 150M) indicating 'Cástaras 1h30/Busquístar 2h', where we immediately climb to the right (Yes, I know!).

The pitted concrete track out of **Notáez** soon gives way to a dirt path climbing past allotments and olive and almond terraces, eventually emerging onto scrubland below the daunting cliffs of **El Celar**. Beyond **El Celar**, we cross an almond grove (possibly ploughed) and immediately bear left onto a narrow path over an embrambled *rambla*.

We then skirt a field of fig saplings and climb through a wilderness of *retama* (this is the GR142, after all!) before passing under some power lines and crossing an *acequia* to join the road from **Cástaras** (Wp.10 195M). Obviously, if you don't want to descend 200-odd metres just to climb again, this road is an alternative route. Equally obviously, it's a lot less attractive.

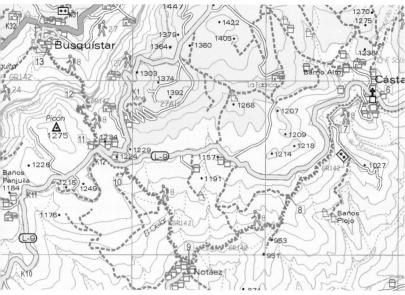

The waypost at Wp.11

Bearing left, we follow the road to the **Trevélez** junction, from where we can see **Busquístar**, which a waypost (Wp.11 199M) claims is one hour away. We leave the road, ignoring the path into the gully and follow the higher path which crosses a slope then descends below the old iron mines of **Cerro del Conjuro**.

After swinging left to cross the gully, the path comes to a rock shelf and begins its extremely dramatic descent into the gorge, following a broad, rocky route down to a bridge over the **Río Trevélez** (Wp.12 220M).

N.B.
A slip path just before the bridge leads to a swimmable pool (concealed by trees and a boulder). More private bathing points can be found by following the path on the right bank upriver to the old electricity installations. From the river, it's a fifteen minute climb to **Busquístar** (Wp.13 240M) along a clear path arriving at the 'Camino al Río /GR142 Notáez 1h30' signs.

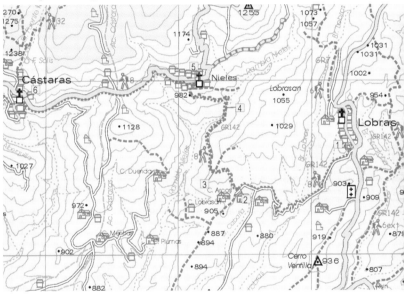

Not the most the most breathtaking of paths (though you may be a bit puffed) and not recommended at the height of the day in summer, but a useful route for long-distance walkers and those wishing to link up with the GR7 (Walk 1) or explore the mountains above **Lanjarón**.

Plaza de la Alpujarra, Órgiva

Access by car: Park just before the BP station at the north-west end of **Órgiva**, where you can usually find a space in the shade.

Stroll
Río Sucio
(Wps. 5-6)

B u s e s b a c k : 1 2 a m , 1 . 3 0 p m , 5.45pm

Passing **Órgiva** BP station, we cross the bridge over the **Río Chico** (Wp.1 0M/km16 of the A-348) and turn right on the GR-421, taking the clear path on the left 50m later (Wp.2 2M). This unmarked path meanders through terraces of olive, orange, lemon and mulberry trees, and passes behind an abandoned factory before joining a partially concreted track (Wp.3 10M) leading onto the A-348 to **Lanjarón**.

The track alongside the Río Sucio

Turning right, we follow the road past the **Venta María** bar to the **Río Sucio** bridge, where we turn right on a waymarked track up the left bank of the river (Wp.4 15M). Shortly after a house shrouded in eucalyptus, the track goes between a waypost (uprooted at the time of writing) and a stone corral with a fig tree (Wp.5 29M), where we bear left into the riverbed then climb the bluffs on the far side. The path (at first clearly waymarked) climbs steadily and then steeply up the western side of the valley toward a large outcrop of rock, the **Rabiete** (Wp.6 54M).

Just before the **Rabiete**, we bear right for a gentler climb past more terraces of olive, almond, and fig trees to come out behind a *cortijo* (Wp.7 66M), usually mapped as the **Cortijo de Meridas** though better known to locals as the **Cortijo de Conde** or **de Tejas** since the *Conde* in question was the only man wealthy enough to roof his house with tiles. The traditional roofing material here is *launa*, a kind of heavy duty daub mixed from the local mica. Unless you want to join the GR7 (see Walk 1, Wp.8), stay above the farm track and bear away from the *cortijo* (W), following the higher traces amid a maze of goat tracks occasionally waymarked with red and/or very old yellow dots.

We continue in this direction staying ten to fifteen metres above a dry watercourse lined with poplars and eucalyptus, following increasingly infrequent and faint yellow dots till a small pond-like reservoir (Wp.8 74M) on our right. After the reservoir, we bear slightly left on the yellow path (WNW) until it joins a dirt track (PF1 Branch C) beside a waypost (Wp.9 81M) a few metres below the GR7 (see Walk 1, Wp.7). We then turn left along the *pista forestal*, which soon reaches a stretch of concrete.

The pond-like reservoir at Wp.8

Just before the concrete ends, we turn right next to a house with a tall weeping willow, the **Venta de los Herradores** (Wp.10 90M). Taking the path behind the house, we rejoin the *pista forestal*, again concreted, which we follow down to a small aqueduct (Wp.11 95M).

Here we bear left and follow a dirt track until it crosses an *acequia* (Wp.12 110M) behind a small *ermita* overlooking **Lanjarón**. On the western side of the *acequia*, we turn right onto a narrow path and zigzag down to rejoin the *pista forestal* into **Lanjarón**, arriving at the road (Wp.13 120M), a few metres from the start of the GR7 to **Cáñar**. We then follow the A-348 into **Lanjarón** where there are plenty of bars, restaurants and hotels. The spa is situated at the western end of town.

10 EL CABALLO

If you only have time for one 3000 metre peak, this is the one to do. It's wilder than the **Mulhacén**, less tiring, more interesting, and quite as 'unique', being the westernmost 3000 metre peak of the chain. However, pathfinding may be a problem in winter and there are frequently strong winds in the summer. The terrain is rough, so don't attempt it in poor conditions.

N.B. Although the start of this itinerary was badly damaged by a forest fire in 2005, the remainder of the walk is sufficiently attractive to justify keeping the route in this edition.

| 4/5 | 4H 50M | 9 km | 900m / 900m | S | 0 |

Access by car: via **Pista Forestal 1**. Park in the turning circle at the end of the *pista forestal*.

> **Stroll**
> **Lanjarón Valley** - stay on the main path after the **Refugio Ventura** to explore the valley.

Pista Forestal 1

From the end of **PF1** (Wp.1 0M), we take the broad wayposted path climbing NW. Ignoring a rough dirt track to the right 50 metres later, we stick to the main path climbing to the partially abandoned but still serviceable **Refugio de Ventura** (Wp.2 21M), from where the **Cerro de Caballo** is clearly visible.

One hundred and fifty metres after the refuge, we leave the main path just before a stand of stubby pine, and bear left at a cairn onto a fainter, rougher path climbing steeply towards the ridge. The path soon crosses an *acequia* (not marked on any maps), above which it continues climbing for 50 metres (NNE) through gorse and spiny broom before levelling out to follow the contour lines of the hillside, crossing the **Barranco de Hiniestral** watercourse and joining a firebreak circling a plantation of pine (Wp.3 49M).

We cross the firebreak and take the path through the woods to their northernmost tip, where the path crosses the firebreak again and heads NE in a clearly visible line across the last stretch of scrub to the first rock slides. Here the landscape changes character. To the south we see something akin to the pasture-rich Pyrenees; to the north is a facsimile of the stony wilderness found in the High Atlas.

The path becomes fainter, rougher and narrower as it climbs (NNE) towards the jagged crags of the **Tajos del Cortadero**, zigzagging through two steep sections and passing a small cairn (Wp.4 105M) before it loses definition beside a green-flanked rivulet just before the **Tajos**.

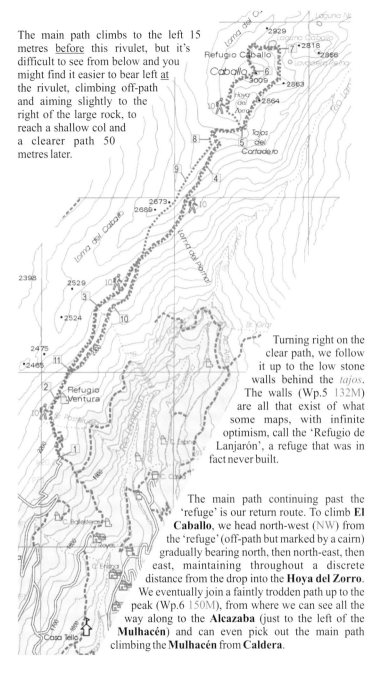

The main path climbs to the left 15 metres <u>before</u> this rivulet, but it's difficult to see from below and you might find it easier to bear left <u>at</u> the rivulet, climbing off-path and aiming slightly to the right of the large rock, to reach a shallow col and a clearer path 50 metres later.

Turning right on the clear path, we follow it up to the low stone walls behind the *tajos*. The walls (Wp.5 132M) are all that exist of what some maps, with infinite optimism, call the 'Refugio de Lanjarón', a refuge that was in fact never built.

The main path continuing past the 'refuge' is our return route. To climb **El Caballo**, we head north-west (NW) from the 'refuge' (off-path but marked by a cairn) gradually bearing north, then north-east, then east, maintaining throughout a discrete distance from the drop into the **Hoya del Zorro**. We eventually join a faintly trodden path up to the peak (Wp.6 150M), from where we can see all the way along to the **Alcazaba** (just to the left of the **Mulhacén**) and can even pick out the main path climbing the **Mulhacén** from **Caldera**.

A clear path descends NW to the **Laguna & Refugio de Caballo** (Wp.7 165M) where a bathe is strongly recommended (always supposing your heart's up to it!) (N.B. bathing in the lagoons is prohibited by the park authorities, a prohibition like most Spanish prohibitions, more often neglected than respected).

El Caballo from the Loma de Cáñar

The return path heads south from the refuge, passing the eastern face of the **Caballo** and the so-called 'Refugio de Lanjarón' to join the top of the path (clearly visible from above) (Wp.8 185M) down to the rivulet. From here you can return to the firebreak/pine-wood by the same route or take a more adventurous, pathless route along the crest (good visibility preferable).

The off-path route follows the line of the ridge, staying just to the east of the rocky outcrops along the crest, until it reaches an outcrop (Wp.9 200M) from where we can see the length of the ridge and, off to the left, the firebreak/pine-wood. We maintain a southerly (S) direction after Wp.9 until we <u>see</u> a large cairn topping another outcrop of rock in the distance. Bearing left to pass below a long, sloping crag, we aim for the northernmost tip of the firebreak/pine-wood, a twenty to thirty minute descent through broom and furze. Alternatively, cut straight down to the outward path from the firebreak/pine-wood.

Ignoring the path taken through the pine on the way up, we follow the firebreak round the lower part of the wood. When it starts climbing on the southern side of the wood (Wp.10 265M), we take the narrow path on the left down to the *acequia*. We then follow the *acequia* till it crosses the path (Wp.11 275M) down to the **Refugio de Ventura** (just before a small pine tree), from where it's a fifteen minute descent back to the car.

Puente Palo is one of the Alpujarras' better kept secrets, which (being cynical about it) might explain why this *Área Recreativa* is so clean. Apart from local walkers and a catatonically taciturn shepherd, it's rare to see anyone there - and yet metre for metre, this is perhaps one of the most beautiful walks in the entire Alpujarras, especially between Wps. 5&8 as it follows the gorgeous **Acequia Grande** under the shade of the finest oak forest in the region. And the miracle of it is, this itinerary appears in no other publication I know of! I can only suppose the want of grandiose views and high peaks means more macho researchers have dismissed it as insignificant.

The view from Puente Palo

During the summer, the extension between **Cañar** and **Cerro Man** has little to recommend it, and should only be taken if you don't have a car; it is, however, a lot of fun on a blustery winter's day. The official start of the walk is **Cerro Man**, though it could equally be started from **Puente Palo Área Recreativa** (Wp.8).

In the following description, **PF2** refers to the main **Pista Forestal 2**, **PF2A** to the **Cáñar** branch.

Though the owner has plans to rebuild, **Cerro Man** is at present no more than a small hump topped with ancient foundations, 4.9km from **Cáñar** on **PF2A**, 3.8km from the junction with the main **PF2**. The track next to it is flanked by two gate-like stone & concrete walls, marking the passage of the dry **Acequia de Barjas**. It's 50 metres from the point where **PF2A** comes alongside the **Acequia Grande** and just above the junction of the two *acequias*.

2 | 1H | 3 km | 300m N | ⟷ | 3*

Strolls

Take **PF2** to **Puente Palo** and, from the bare slope to the south of the *Área Recreativa* (Wp.8), take the chained driveway down to the path on the right of the white-painted house then follow the *acequia* till you reach a wire fence above a reservoir (**Wp.5**), bear right and take the dirt tracks back to the *Área Recreativa*.

Also see **Pista Forestal 2**.

(* in **Cáñar**, though refreshments <u>may</u> be available when **Cortijo La Muda** is open to the public - see Appendix A, Pista Forestal 2 & Appendix C, Fernando Vilchez)

Access by car: you can park beside the track at Wp.1.

Extension
(3 walker, 1½ hours return, 3 kilometres, ascents 400 metres, descents
400 metres)

Take the concrete lane climbing from the western side of **Cánar** church.
Ignore a rock-laid path climbing left above orange garage doors and take
the second path on the left, directly in line with the church tower and just
after a concrete building on the right immersed in fig trees. The dirt path
soon turns into a mule trail that climbs straight up, cutting across and
occasionally disappearing into **PF2A** five times before it reaches **Cerro
Man**. For ease of reference these crossings are numbered in brackets in the
following section.

After 5 minutes we take the access track behind a large fenced *cortijo* to join
the **PF2A** for the first time (**1**). We bear left here and then again 100 metres
later, on a rough track alongside another fenced *cortijo*.

Crossing this second *cortijo*'s access track next to a *Prohibido El Paso* sign,
we recover the mule trail as it winds up alongside a dry watercourse, to
cross the **PF2A** (**2**) just below a scattered group of scorched chestnuts, and
again 75 metres later (**3**). Immediately after this third crossing the path runs
into another access track, climbing past a small house above which it
rejoins the **PF2A** (**4**). 5 metres to the left we recover a paved section of the
mule trail, climbing behind a ruin and a small stone cabin.

30 metres behind the cabin we cross the **PF2A** for the last time (**5**) and
climb straight up, passing between a stand of holm oak on the edge of the
PF2A (on our right) and a long grassy meadow (on our left). The ruins and
large threshing circle of **Cerro Man** are 75 metres above the holm oak, 40
minutes (at a rapid pace) from **Cañar**.

From Cerro Man
From Cerro Man (Wp.1 0M), after following **PF2A** for 200 metres we cross a
branch (often dry) of the **Acequia Alta** leading down, on our right, to a line of
chestnut trees descending to the **Cortijo las Alberquillas**. 20 metres later
(Wp.2 3M), we leave the dirt track and turn left onto a rough path marked by a
cairn.

The path climbs parallel to the *acequia* before emerging in a field (probably
ploughed) in front of a single-storey cabin set amid newly planted poplar and
willow trees. We cross the field and bear left above the house onto a path
winding into a small chestnut wood, where it broadens to a rough dirt track,
climbing steadily until an easier gradient across another field approaches a
junction between the *acequia* and **PF2A**.

We follow **PF2A** for 20 metres till it bears right and we take a very rough dirt
track climbing to the left (Wp.3 15M). This track climbs steadily, gradually
bearing back towards the *acequia* to join another, better stabilised track
leading to a carefully fenced *cortijo*, where we take the path to the left of the
house between the *acequia* and the fence.

We follow this path as it crosses a series of shallow terraced fields and widens
to a rough dirt track before climbing gently to rejoin **PF2A** (Wp.4 25M).

The Acequia Grande, between Wps. 5&8

We then follow **PF2A** past several houses, at the end of which, just where the fence bears right above a large empty reservoir, we leave the dirt track to join a path along the **Acequia Grande** (Wp.5 30M).

We now follow the *acequia* path all the way to **Puente Palo**, ignoring junctions with driveways at Wps. 6 (40M) and **7** (50M) until we come to a white-painted house with a well-tended garden. The driveway behind the house brings us up to the denuded platform just south of **Puente Palo Área Recreativa** (Wp.8 55M).

This route is so lovely, you'll probably want to return the same way, but if you insist on a circuit, take **PF2** south to **PF2A** (Wp.9) and follow **PF2A** back to **Cerro Man** (5km from Wp.9).

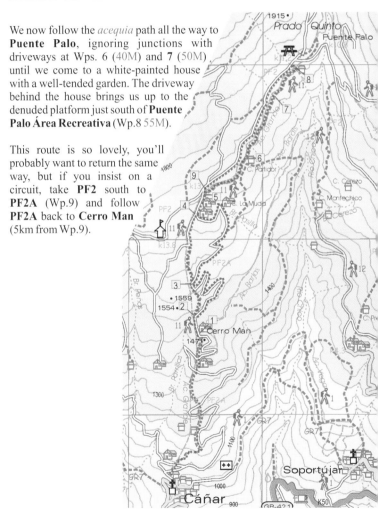

Often as not PRs are no more than a tardy acknowledgement of what dedicated walkers have known for decades, moving connoisseurs to mutter about grandmothers and sucking eggs, but in this instance the pathmakers have done us proud and the **PR22** is a genuinely pioneering route, refurbishing a little known arboretum path dating from the 1920s reforestation programme.

Fine views en route towards Loma de Cáñar

Despite being a linear two way route, it's a thoroughly stimulating itinerary through lovely woodland with fine views and plenty of great picnic spots, and is particularly recommended in Autumn when the leaves are turning and the *robledal* on the western flank of the *barranco* is splashed with patches of gold and red. The first stretch, which corresponds to the stroll, is recommended to anyone with a fondness for wild fruits as one can gather crab apples, berries of the *madroño* (strawberry tree), plus chestnuts and walnuts. The route is well wayposted and very simple to follow, so description is purely for the purposes of pacing progress.

This is a two-way linear route.

| 4 | 2¼ H | 8 km | 405m / 405m | ⟺ | 0 |

Extension	**Stroll:** to Wp.3
If you don't intend driving to **Puente Palo**, you might wish to turn the walk into a circuit, returning via **PF2** (a 10km loop). However, given that the track is eminently driveable and much driven, this is only recommended on a wild and blustery autumn day or in mid winter, when the route may be laced with snow.	**Easy Version** Anyone accompanied by a non-walking driver might like to do the walk as a linear descent.

Access by car:
To reach the start, take **PF2** from the **Ermita de Padre Eterno** and park just below the hairpin bend at km4.7, 350 metres after the end of the tarmac.

The walk starts on the branch track off to the left marked with a mapboard outlining the route (Wp.1 0M). 50 metres

The mapboard at Wp.1

behind the mapboard, we pass a small cabin (crab apple and *madroño* on your left), after which our track winds along a balcony lined with walnut and chestnut trees, bringing into view **Cerillo Redondo** (see Walk 14).

Ignoring a fork descending to the left (Wp.2 10M), we continue on the main track till it doubles back to the right below **Barranco Cerezo** (Wp.3 16M), at which point we take a minor track to the left, initially on the level then climbing steadily through mixed woodland. When the track curves right toward a gated entrance to **Cortijo Montechico**, we again fork left (Wp.4 22M) continuing on a broad trail climbing steadily to steeply.

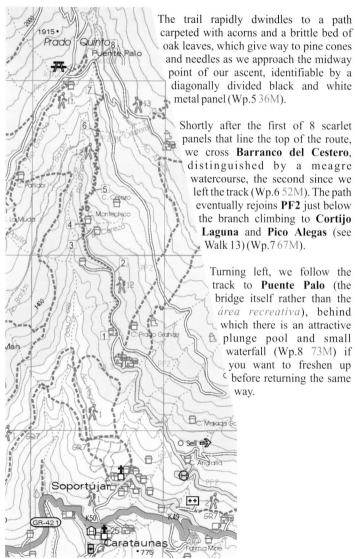

The trail rapidly dwindles to a path carpeted with acorns and a brittle bed of oak leaves, which give way to pine cones and needles as we approach the midway point of our ascent, identifiable by a diagonally divided black and white metal panel (Wp.5 36M).

Shortly after the first of 8 scarlet panels that line the top of the route, we cross **Barranco del Cestero**, distinguished by a meagre watercourse, the second since we left the track (Wp.6 52M). The path eventually rejoins **PF2** just below the branch climbing to **Cortijo Laguna** and **Pico Alegas** (see Walk 13) (Wp.7 67M).

Turning left, we follow the track to **Puente Palo** (the bridge itself rather than the *área recreativa*), behind which there is an attractive plunge pool and small waterfall (Wp.8 73M) if you want to freshen up before returning the same way.

13 PUENTE PALO - PICO ALEGAS - PUENTE PALO

Pico Alegas, as seen from Loma de Cáñar

A relatively easy high-mountain walk though complicated by a section where the path is so badly overgrown one's obliged to plunge through the overhanging boughs of pine trees. It's well worth the effort, though. The spectacle of the high-peaks is fabulous, the ridge gives an unusual perspective on the **Poqueira Gorge**, **Pico de las Alegas** itself is a lovely, little-visited spot, and the descent enjoys superb views of the **Contraviessa**, the **Sierra de Lújar** and, to the west, the **Axarquia**, all against a backdrop of the Mediterranean. Beware of improvising your own routes up to **Cebollar** (Wp.16) - I've tried them all and this remains the simplest!

Access by car:
Access via **Pista Forestal 2** or Walk 11 or 12. Park in the shade on the *pista forestal* to the east of Wp.1.

Suggested Strolls
(a) Short Version to Wp.5 (3 walker, 2½ hour return)
(b) Also see **Pista Forestal 2**

The *pico*, from Pista Forestal 2

From the western end of **Puente Palo Área Recreativa** we take the chained dirt track (Wp.1 0M) north (N). We follow the track as it climbs steadily through the pine forest, ignoring all branches on the left and taking the third branch (fourth in reality, but the third clear one) on the right (Wp.3 35M).

N.B.
Beware - the second branch on the right (Wp.2 20M) has precisely the same configuration in relation to the main track as Wp.3 and crosses the same watercourse lower down to enter the lower half of the **Vivero de los**

Waypoint 3

Helechares. Wp.3 is distinguished by three small cairns and some faint, ancient waymarks; **Refugio Cebollar** is visible high up to our right.

The branch track crosses a watercourse to join another dirt track climbing alongside the *vivero*. We bear left, ignoring a branch to the right and cross a rough wire gate to enter the *vivero*.

We then follow this track all the way to the river, ignoring all branches and sticking to the main traces all the time.

En route, the track climbs gently towards a stand of sickly looking pine, bringing us within sight of the pale grey walls of the **Cebollar Refuge** and the rocks along the western edge of **Pico Alegas**. 5 minutes after the stand of sickly looking pine, the track enters a long S-bend, at the top of which (Wp.4 70M) it levels out: it's worth pausing here to get your bearings for the way up to the refuge.

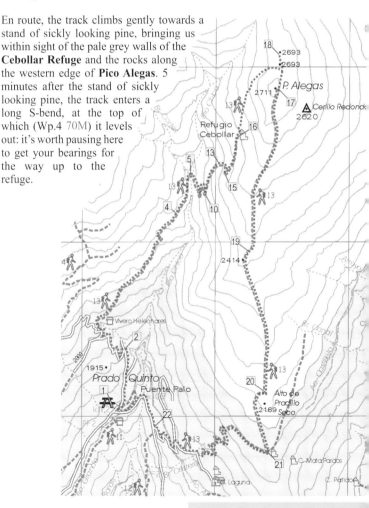

It looks a relatively simple ascent, zigzagging up the slope before bearing left (Wp.10) to cross the pinewood, after which it climbs towards the rocky outcrop above the pinewood (Wp.15) where a clear path leads to the refuge. However, the path is very badly overgrown and, if the authorities don't do anything or not enough eccentrics like you and me come blundering through, it'll probably disappear altogether in the next few years. The first tricky point comes at the end of the second long leftward bearing stretch of zigzag, where the path all but disappears in the woods (Wp.9). Take care not to continue into the woods, but double back to the right in order to cross the wood along the higher line of pines.

N.B. Most of the cairns between Wps.6 & 15 have been built by me - all subsequent contributions gratefully received! Because there are so many of them, not all these waypoints are marked on the map. *Wps.6-15 are timed from the river.

Soon after Wp.4 the track crosses another wire gate, leaving the *vivero* and descending to the waymarked ford across the Río Chico (Wp.5 80M) to join the path up to the woods.

Fungus in the woods

*At the first rocky outcrop 100 metres from the river, we leave the main traces and bear left on a rough path marked by two cairns *(Wp.6 3M) to climb steadily to another cairn (Wp.7 5M) beside a shallow boulder-strewn gully.

We turn left here along a stretch where the path virtually disappears in furze and broom, maintaining a northerly direction to pass just above another cairn and a large rocky outcrop (Wp.8 7M) beyond which a very faint path passes to the right of the first pine and, at another large cairn (Wp.9 10M), doubles-back on the right in a SE direction.

After climbing to the left of a few more pines, this very faint path disappears briefly, but soon reappears to climb to another large cairn (Wp.10 12M). The clearer path continues in a SE direction, but we bear sharp left and go to the right of the next line of pine to cross the pinewood.

The way is often confused and frequently invaded by pine (anyone with a chainsaw in their backpack could make themselves very popular indeed), but if at every apparent Y-junction, you bear right and ALWAYS TAKE THE UPPER TRACES (even when the lower ones seem clearer), you should find cairns at Wp.11 (19M) and Wp.12 (23M) before emerging beyond the main wood in a shallow gully marked by three cairns (Wp.13 27M).

N.B.
If there are no cairns when you emerge from the wood, you're probably lower down, in which case you have a very steep climb zigzagging up to the refuge.

At Wp.13, we bear right and climb straight up the gully (there's no path) then turn right at another cairn (Wp.14 30M) to follow a reasonably clear path climbing gently along the topside of the wood. Just before the rocky outcrop noted at Wp.4, we bear sharp left at another cairn (Wp.15 33M) from where we can see the refuge again, a couple of hundred metres ahead.

Unfortunately, there's another small stand of pine to be negotiated, this one devastated by storms and demanding some delicate manoeuvring to clamber over felled trunks, but the way is at least obvious and soon leads to the refuge (Wp.16 43M [185M from Wp.1]), a badly weathered concrete shell but clean enough for sleeping rough, and welcome shelter in bad weather. There's a small spring to the NW of the refuge.

Contrary to what some maps tell you, there's no clear path between the refuge and the peak, though there are occasional better trodden sections. Heading in a northerly direction towards the last scattered rocks along the ridge, we gradually bear north-east to join a reasonably clear section through the rocks, though that in turn gradually loses definition before disappearing altogether.

Maintaining a north-easterly direction, we emerge on the ridge 50 metres north of the official peak (Wp.17 205M) and 100 metres south of some stone windbreaks (Wp.18) - welcome shelter when the wind's blowing, which it often is, and in any case a cosy picnic spot.

The way back (much simpler than the way up, but a dull climb) follows what's left of the old **Cañada Real** (S), a dirt track (faint at first but soon becoming clearer) running along the ridge past a series of tall cross-country skiing cairns before descending to merge with a firebreak (Wp.19 240M). After a steady descent, the firebreak climbs a hummock, the **Alto de Pradillo Seco**, just before which another dirt track (Wp.20 260M) bears right to skirt the hummock and join a broader dirt track (Wp.21 270M), which we take to the right, to descend to **Pista Forestal 2** (Wp.22 310M) ten minutes from **Puente Palo**.

The first time we tried this route, we turned back, defeated by our failure to find what a rather sketchy Spanish description dubbed a 'trail'. It was only when we later realized no 'trail' existed and the description was sketchy because its authors hadn't actually done the walk, that we were emboldened to go back and have another bash. Take that as a warning. Despite beginning and ending on dirt tracks, this is a largely pathless walk and is only suitable for those who positively enjoy getting well off the beaten track.

That said, the rewards are remarkable, with great views, a real sense of high mountain adventure, and a degree of isolation that is likely to be complete save for the local shepherd and the odd Spanish hiker doing a traverse of the entire *sierra*. It's very dry and exposed though, and is not recommended in hot weather or when visibility is poor.

Access: by car

Short Version: see Wp.7

We start as per Walk 13 on the track climbing to the north from the western end of **Puente Palo Área Recreativa** (Wp.1 0M). Sticking to the main track and ignoring all branches, including (Wp.2 31M) the cairn marked turning on the right for **Pico Alegas**, we climb steadily across the pine covered slopes of **Prado Quinto**.

Toward the top of the woods, the track describes a long level southerly arc before doubling back at a junction distinguished by faint blue waymarks (Wp.3 47M), after which we resume our steady ascent. Climbing clear of the more closely planted trees, we see what appears to be a stone cabin with a green door, in fact one wing of the shepherd's corral that marks the start of our off-path antics.

Fine views open out behind us over the **Guadalfeo** valley and the **Contraviessa** as we continue zigzagging up the track till we reach the corral. Directly behind the building, a shallow watershed points toward a distinct, bare conical summit, pricked with a nipple-like cairn. This is the smaller of the two summits on the **Loma de Cáñar** that go by the name of **Cerillo Redondo** and is the culminating point of the present itinerary.

To reach the top, we turn left behind the corral, leaving the remains of the track in order to climb along the right bank (left hand side as we ascend) of the shallow watershed (Wp.4 75M). Goat pellets and the odd better-trodden patches of bare earth suggest this is the way taken by the local shepherd, but as usual, the goats go every-which-way so take this as already being off-path. For the sake of descriptive convenience (the walking could as well be done either side), we stick to the right bank of the watershed, climbing steeply to its 'source' where it bifurcates on a shallow grassy platform (Wp.5 92M).

We follow the fork to the left and continue climbing (N), passing a cairn on a large rock 100 metres later (Wp.6). Bearing slightly right toward the line of crags on our right, we climb across very rough, natural terracing, bringing **Cerillo Redondo** back into view as we weave our way through a wall of stubby pine.

On the far side of the pine, looking up toward **Cerillo Redondo** and the head of the crags on our right, we can see a patch of clear path

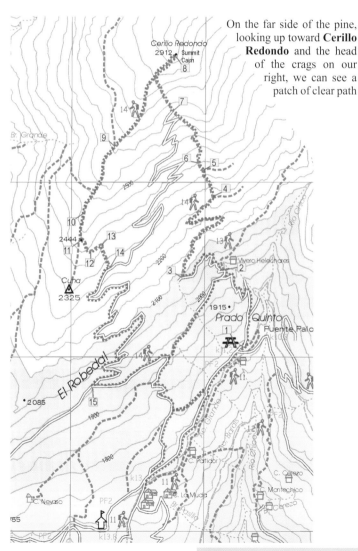

and, to it's left, the last zigzags of a dirt track that climbs from **El Robledal**, the oak forest south of **Puente Palo**. Roughly following the course of a dry watershed, we climb steeply (NNW) to follow the patch of 'clear' path (not so obvious once you're on it), until it joins the end of the dirt track (Wp.7 129M). If you've got this far and suddenly concluded 'off-path' is not your thing, this track is your escape route, rejoining the described itinerary at Wp.14.

Descending along the crest of the ridge

Crossing the end of the track, we climb toward the lower crag immediately south of **Cerillo Redondo**, picking our way across the debris-strewn slopes, taking advantage of the more path-like patches of grit between the bulkier debris. This is hard going and toward the end you maybe wondering whether it's worth the effort, but I assure you it is.

As we pass to the right of the lower crag, a significant lump of rock itself from close up, **Caballo** comes into view and, on the final stretch up to the pillar cairn on **Cerillo Redondo** (Wp.8 162M), a fabulous vista opens out including **Tajo de los Machos**, **Veleta** and **Mulhacén**.

Piedra de los Pájaros

Retracing our steps to the lower crag, we pick our way along the ridge, still off-path, bringing into view the clear line of a narrow path about a kilometre to the south. How you reach this path rather depends on which views you favour, west or east, but either way, it's a relatively easy descent as we make our way along one flank of the ridge or the other avoiding the more obtrusive central crags. The views are superb, particularly over the **Contraviessa** and, to the west, the **Axarquía**.

Aiming for the little cluster of rocks at what appears to be the lip of the ridge, we join the clear, narrow path seen from above (Wp.9 184M 2622m). If you need a windbreak, the cluster of rocks 300 metres later is probably your best bet on this route. In an emergency, 200 metres SE of these rocks there is a shelter built into the rock, though I haven't actually visited it, so I don't know what state this is in.

The path peters out as we descend from the first cluster of rocks, but soon becomes clear again as we approach the next cluster, **Piedra de los Pájaros**, and the line of scorched earth (Wp.10 200M) marking the recent fire damage that moved us to replace the ascent to the **Casa Forestal de Tello** with the present itinerary.

The original path descended along the western flank of the ridge past the **Cuna** rocks, but this is now such a desolate landscape, I recommend one final off-path stretch. 225 metres into the patchy scorched scrub, we turn left behind **Piedra de los Pájaros** (Wp.11 205M), descending off the ridge and off-path toward a clear dirt track above **El Robledal**, the same track crossed at Wp.7.

After passing between a gateway of red and grey rock (Wp.12 210M), we swing left (NE) traversing rough, rocky ground to join the end of a new firebreak branching off the track we saw from above (Wp.13 213M). From hereon, the walking is considerably easier.

Following the firebreak down to the dirt track (Wp.14 218M), we turn right and embark on a infinitely gentle descent, snaking down the hillside, each switchback offering an alternative outlook. Shortcuts are possible, but probably not terribly desirable at this stage, so I recommend staying on the track. Eventually, after more hairpins than an upmarket salon, we pass a row of beehives and reach a junction (Wp.15 270M), where we turn left to continue on the main track as it runs parallel to the upper limit of **El Robledal**. We stick to this track as it drops down to descend through the oak forest, eventually joining **PF2** at the junction with **PF2A** (Wp.16 305M), where we turn left to return to the *área recreativa*.

The catchphrase claims 'the old ones are the best' and, in this classic tour of the **Poqueira** valley, an adage coined for comedy holds true for walking. Our new version of the itinerary, adapted to avoid a fence erected after publication of the previous edition, is a figure of eight that can be done in its entirety or divided into two shorter loops, both of which would make very satisfactory short excursions.

Access: on foot from any of the three villages.

Pampaneira is such a maze, describing the way out of it might constitute a walk description in itself. To simplify matters, from the entrance to the village, take the lane in front of **Hostal Ruta de Mulhacen** and climb at every junction until you pass **Calle Real** and see, off to your left, **Calle Rosario**, at the end of which is a 'Camino de Bubíon' signpost (Wp.1 9M).

> ### Stroll
> **Pozo de Pampaneira** - take **Calle Princesa** from the **Pampaneira** car park, pass the **Carnicería Mercedes** and, when you see the 'Calle Silencio' sign, turn left to join a concrete track (**Calle Moraleda**) descending to the main road and the track into the valley.
>
> **Short Versions**: either of the loops

Waypoint 1

We follow the paved *camino* as it climbs through **Calle Castillo**, at the top of which we fork left below houses Nºs 1 and 3, as indicated by a waypost. Traversing well-tended terraces, we fork right at the next junction (waymarked and wayposted) (Wp.2 15M) and climb steadily along a cobbled mule trail below a malodorous dog pound.

Just below the pound, we briefly join a track before recovering the old mule trail (Wp.3 19M). Climbing steadily along a chestnut fringed dirt trail, we enter **Bubíon** via the **Fuente Barrio Bajo** (Wp.4 34M).

Climbing past a 'GR7' signpost, we cut cross the church square then follow the sign for 'Camino del Río/Los Cortijos/Polideportivo Municipal'. At the northeastern corner of the municipal football field, we take a broad trail marked with a waypost (Wp.5 40M). Ignoring minor branches accessing fields and huts, we descend to cross **Barranco de Tejar**, immediately after which we pass a new trail climbing to the right (Wp.6 47M). Sticking to the old trail as it descends towards the river, we cross **Barranco de Armuña**, 50 metres after which we reach the point where the loops of our figure of eight intersect, a signposted turning on the right for 'Capileira' (Wp.7 58M).

We descend to **Puente Molino**, a great spot for a picnic, beyond which we climb to a T-junction, where the two loops diverge (Wp.8 65M). Turning right, we climb past **Cortijo Enrique** (much barking, mostly benign and, if not benign, timid) and cross an ancient *acequia* layered with black pipes (Wp.9 72M).

After passing an abandoned cabin and a threshing circle, we fork right at the enbrambled carcass of a dead tree (Wp.10 75M), and follow a good level path along a contour into the **Barranco de las Rosas**. After crossing a first watercourse, we bear right at a wayposted junction of paths in a second watercourse (Wp.11 80M), taking either of the forks immediately after the watercourse (they rejoin almost immediately on the bend of a broader trail).

Following a brief climb, the trail levels out, passing below a small cabin and bringing into view on the right bank the yellowish walls of **Cortijo de la Sacristia**, which stands above **Puente Chiscar**. At a wayposted junction below two small *cortijos* (Wp.12 93M), we fork right, descending to the picturesque **Puente Chiscar**.

Back on the left bank of the river, we follow a broad mule trail, climbing steadily to a junction just below **Cortijo de la Sacristia** where we turn right (Wp.13 100M).

The view north after Wp.13

Climbing steadily to steeply, we enter **Capileira** via a concrete track, signposted 'Puente Chistal' and 'Puente Chiscal' (sic) (Wp.14 115M).

A corner house in Capileira

We initially follow the concrete track, then carry straight on at the first bend where the main track doubles back into the village. When the concrete runs into a cobbled alley, we turn right then bear left in front of **Casa Liliana** and pass under a succession of *tinaos* (see Walk 3 Wp.8). At the far end of **Plaza Vieja**, we turn right and descend to the signposted 'Camino de las Higuerillas / Molino de Bubión' (Wp.15 120M).

After a level stretch, the path descends rapidly, intermittently shadowing a torrent before cutting away toward a two-tiered cabin and descending back to

Wp.7 (135M), from where we retrace our steps to Wp.8 (142M). Turning left, we climb steadily to a Y-junction at the stump of a fire-scorched chestnut tree (151M), where we bear left.

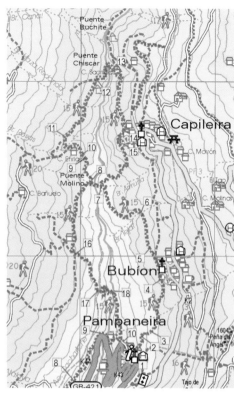

After crossing three watercourses, the second two usually dry, we climb through an oak forest to the grassy terraces below a ruin, beyond which a waypost indicates our path down to the **Pozo de Pampaneira** (Wp.16 160M).

The path traverses more woodland then emerges in the open and descends past a fissured pillar of rock. At a wayposted junction immediately after a roofless cabin (Wp.17 174M), we double back to the left and zigzag down to the bridge below the **Pozo de Pampaneira**.

On the far side of the bridge, we turn right on a narrow dirt track (Wp.18 180M) which leads to a bend in the main road, where the concrete lane of the GR7 climbs into **Pampaneira** via **Calle Moraleda** and **Calle Princesa**.

16 PAMPANEIRA - PITRES - PAMPANEIRA

A complex route of contrasts, following some very steep stairs, some very tame forestry tracks, and some very rough cross country-walking! The stairway between Wps. 4&5 is not recommended in the opposite direction unless you take a perverse pleasure in vertigo. The end and start of this walk have recently been waymarked as a *sendero local*.

*   5 for the stairs, 2 for everything else
**   **Pampaneira - Pitres** 2½ hours
            Pitres - Pampaneira 1 hour 35 mins
            Circuit without **Pitres** 3¼ hours
***   from **Pitres** - 100m

> **Short Version**
> Turn right at Wp.9 rather than descending to **Pitres**.

Buses back:
         from **Pitres** - 3.30pm / 6pm
         from **Pampaneira** - 2.05pm / 7.20pm

Our itinerary starts at **Pampaneira** cemetery, accessible by a concrete track on the left 200 metres above the town limits. If there's no room to park here, start from the upper car-park on the GR-421 and take **Calle La Peseta** below the brown garage doors on the hairpin bend. Cross the porch of house N°1 onto **Calle Real** and follow this *calle* up to the cemetery.

From the cemetery gates (Wp.1 0M), we continue on the concrete track, climbing past a wayposted slip path doubling back toward the football field. When the concrete track itself doubles back to the right, we carry straight on along a dirt track leading to a white water hut, immediately after which we turn right on a narrow, unmarked path climbing steeply into the oak wood (Wp.2 5M).

The path briefly joins the interred *tubería* feeding **Pampaneira** power station before forking right and climbing to a staggered junction crossing the **Bubíon** road (Wp.3 14M).

We continue climbing steeply to a waymarked T-junction, where we turn left (Wp.4 19M). 50 metres later, we rejoin the *tubería* above the first set of stairs and turn right (Wp.5 20M) to begin the long slog up to the holding dam. At the holding dam, we duck under the pipe (Wp.6 40M) and follow a faint trail across the shale toward a square concrete triangulation post.

The *tubería* and stair

The path bears right shortly before the post and climbs to join the **GR7** (Walk 3, Wp.3). We bear right here, away from the GR, on a path climbing SSE to pass below the dam wall and join the dirt track up to the **Tajo de Soju** (see **PF3** strolls).

Just before a small metal pylon mounted with **Pampaneira**'s TV aerials (the *mirador* is 200 metres beyond the turning circle behind these aerials), we bear left to follow the track NE towards the rocky outcrop of the **Peña del Angel**. On the far side of the **Barranco de la Sangre** (on our right) is the 'graveyard' of concrete pipes (Walk 3 Wp.5), looking curiously like an experiment in installation art from this angle.

The track crosses both the old GR7 (two wayposts, Wp.7 55M) and the new route (Walk 3, Wp.4). You can either cross the **Barranco de la Sangre** here (to Walk 3's Wp.5), or stay on the track past the transformer towers till the Y-junction (Wp.8 61M). At the Y-junction, we turn sharp right to follow the 'Cortijo Prado Toro' signs (SE), crossing the **GR7** again (Walk 3, Wp.5) after five minutes.

Ignoring all branches, we follow the main track down towards **Prado Toro**. At the next signposted turning to 'Cortijo Prado Toro' (Wp.9 75M), we stay on the main track as it bears right to descend past a second left-hand branch before passing above a vineyard and below a turning on the right (Wp.10 86M). This turning is the return route, which can be taken now for a circuit lasting a little over three hours.

To continue to **Pitres**, ignore branches leading to the vineyard (on the left) and something that looks suspiciously like a tip (on the right), and stick to the main track as it bears left. We leave the track at the sharp right-hand bend round the heliport (Wp.11 95M) and continue (E) on a path skirting an orchard to a junction with a dirt track (Wp.12 101M). We then follow this dirt track (E), crossing a torrent (Wp.13 107M) before gradually descending to join the road (Wp.14 110M) down to **Pitres**, arriving in front of the **Disco Pub El Patio** (Wp.15 121M) just short of the bars in the main *plaza*. To return to **Pampaneira**, retrace your steps until Wp. 9.

To start from Pitres
If you're starting from **Pitres**, take the road in front of the *alimentación* Spar and climb past the **Pub El Patio**, the school and **Casa Holandesa**. After a steep S-bend, ignore the tarmac road to the right and the driveway on the left,

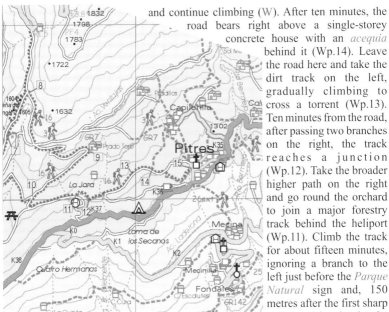

and continue climbing (W). After ten minutes, the road bears right above a single-storey concrete house with an *acequia* behind it (Wp.14). Leave the road here and take the dirt track on the left, gradually climbing to cross a torrent (Wp.13). Ten minutes from the road, after passing two branches on the right, the track reaches a junction (Wp.12). Take the broader higher path on the right and go round the orchard to join a major forestry track behind the heliport (Wp.11). Climb the track for about fifteen minutes, ignoring a branch to the left just before the *Parque Natural* sign and, 150 metres after the first sharp right-hand bend, take the track on the left (Wp.10, 35 minutes from **Pitres**).

To Pampaneira from Wp.10

The clear, well-stabilized track climbs past a large empty reservoir before descending to cross the **Barranco de la Sangre** and climbing again to pass another narrower track doubling back on the right (Wp.16, 45 minutes from **Pitres**) to the **GR7**.

Fine views south over the Sierra Mecina en route

Continue on the main track but don't spend too much time admiring the fine views of the southern *sierras* (though do keep your eye open for a big buck *cabra montés* that's often to be seen round here; deeply puzzled by a human presence, he lets ramblers come quite close) since you need to be alert for path finding here as the itinerary soon leaves the dirt track and descends to a firebreak.

One hundred metres from Wp.16 the track bears right, away from the **Barranco de la Sangre**; up to our right is a large sail-like rock below which an outcrop of rock marks the descent from the track. In a further fifty metres the track bears right, just before the sail-like rock (now concealed by holm oak), the track widens slightly and we turn left between (hopefully!) two cairns (Wp.17 50M) onto a very rough bulldozer trail passing between two stands of spindly holm oak (five on the left, nine or ten on right). If the cairns have been destroyed, you might be able to identify the spot by some large pieces of plastic moulding that have been dumped there.

The bulldozer trail bears left and descends on the right of the small outcrop of rock, within sight of the firebreak below. The track gets even rougher (!) and, just after the outcrop of rock, passes a small sturdy pine tree on our left, where the trail gets too steep and slippery for an easy descent. To avoid the indignity of doing this section on your bottom, bear right (SW) after the sturdy pine and immediately before a stand of very small holm oaks, and follow the faint goat tracks that head towards two pine trees, one little, one large, after which it's a relatively easy descent to the firebreak (Wp.18 59M).

We then follow the firebreak (W) for one hundred metres as it dips below a stand of tall pines. Just as it starts to climb gently, we leave the firebreak to take a narrow goat track (Wp.19 62M) marked by two cairns (please feel free to add a stone) and a forked pine log. We follow this track as it runs parallel to the firebreak above.

Just after two bushy holm oaks, the track splinters. We follow the upper traces which appear to climb slightly towards the firebreak, then duck under the next holm oak where the main path becomes clearer again. After another cairn, the path descends gently, passing below the skeletons of two burned pine trees and, five minutes from the firebreak, above the ruins of a tiny hut, a few minutes from the **Hoya de los Guardas** pass into the **Poqueira** valley (Wp.20 71M).

If you are doing this route in reverse
If you're doing this route in reverse, the climb from the pass to the firebreak is easy to find, but locating the bulldozer traces is tricky as they don't go all the way to the firebreak. Follow the firebreak east (E) for one hundred and fifty metres till it starts a gentle descent into the **Barranco de la Sangre** and you can see its continuation climbing the eastern side of the *barranco* above a newly planted vineyard. Just before the firebreak drops dramatically into the valley, you'll see a cairn on an outcrop of rock on your right. Ten metres before that cairn, another larger one on the left marks the bottom of the bulldozer track (Wp. 21), which climbs very steeply up to the left of another outcrop of rock, after which the way to the forestry track at Wp.16 becomes clearer.

From the **Hoya de los Guardas** pass (Wp.21), a clear path crosses the flank of the **Monte de Pampaneira** (NNW) into the **Poqueira** gorge. After ten minutes, the path passes some beehives and widens into a track descending to the **Bubíon** road. We cross the road and follow the clear goat tracks down to the sports field and the concrete track into **Pampaneira** (95M).

17 CAPILEIRA - LA CEBADILLA - CAPILEIRA

This is the well-known **Red Route** from **Capileira** to **La Cebadilla**, the abandoned hamlet built to service the Central **Poqueira** power-station at the junction of the **Ríos Toril** & **Naute**. On the way back, we pass **Puente Buchite**, one of the loveliest picnic spots in the gorge, but get there early if you're visiting in the summer, as it's popular with local expats and guided parties. If it's not your habit already, take a towel. You can park in the municipal car-park or, if you don't fancy negotiating the narrow alley down to the car-park, on the main road one hundred metres above the **Café-Bar Rosendo**.

* + 20 minutes for the extension   ** in **Capileira**

Strolls
(a) La Cebadilla-Río Naute
Drive to **La Cebadilla** on the dirt track starting at km2.7 of **Pista Forestal 3**, then stroll upriver from **Puente Hondero**.
(b) Capileira-Puente Buchite
From the **Mirador de Aldeire** follow the track down to the branch path to **Puente Buchite**.
(c) Capileira - Acequia de los Lugares - Mirador Aldeire - Capileira
From the *Aparcamiento Municipal* sign in **Capileira (Wp.1)** follow the road up to the picnic spot above the village. Take the dirt track on the left. Bear right at the Y-junction, then left to head for the round building. Bear right onto the **Cebadilla** route. Leave the path where two tracks merge next to the **Acequia de los Lugares** and bear left to follow a degraded path (W) down a watercourse along a ridge behind a *cortijo* to the tip of the ridge. Thread your way off-path through the rocks to the south to pick up a faint path running up to some fields, then take the narrow path descending to the **Mirador de Aldeire**.

Starting at the northern end of **Capileira**, we take the slip road next to the *Aparcamiento Municipal* sign just past the **Café-Bar Rosendo**, then bear left on the **Caidero de las Ramones** and turn right opposite the *fuente* on a cobbled path (Wp.1 0M).

Waypoint 1

Climbing past the mapboards, we cross a dirt track at the edge of the village and take the broad path past a Blue Route mapboard. This path passes two

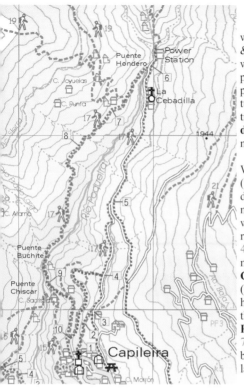

water huts (Wps. 2&3, 10M & 15M): after the first hut, we continue up the main path towards the electricity pylons; after the second, we turn left on a narrow dirt track leading to the **Acequia de Lugares** at a waypost and new stone building.

We then follow the *acequia* (which occasionally disappears underground, notably where the track widens near a recently restored *cortijo* ([Wp.4 40M]) till a gentle five minute climb leads to **La Cebadilla** forestry track (Wp.5 50M). We turn left here and follow the track through **La Cebadilla** to the **Puente Hondero** (Wp.6 70M), passing above a fine bathing spot just after the last buildings on the left.

Approaching La Cebadilla

Extension
From **Puente Hondero**, take the concrete track behind the red and white barrier, cross a second bridge at the junction of the **Ríos Toril** and **Naute**, and a third, **Puente Naute**, to a *Parque Natural* mapboard (see Walk 18). When the path upriver bears left and starts

Puente Hondero

climbing, carry straight on to descend to the river and a pleasant bathing spot, ten minutes from **Puente Hondero**.

To return to Capileira
To return to **Capileira**, we take the track climbing south from **Puente Hondero** along the right bank of the **Río Poqueira**. After ten minutes of steady climbing, the track bears sharp right below a *cortijo* (Wp.7 80M). Immediately after the bend, a waypost indicates a narrow path climbing between the main farm

buildings and a tall pylon with a small aerial on top. We follow this path between the fields beyond the *cortijo* until it goes to the left of a ruin and joins the **Blue Route**.

Continuing on the lower **Red Route**, we eventually cross a small torrent among poplar trees, where the path divides. The branches soon merge again, but in dry weather it's probably nicer to take the lower path along the stream. Once the paths rejoin, we climb beside a narrow, cement-lined *acequia* to a small bridge over another torrent, after which a muddy stretch and a brief climb lead to another *acequia* and waypost (Wp.8 95M).

After another *cortijo*, evidently a goat farm, the path bears round to cross two gates and a *barranco*. We ignore the tracks climbing beyond the *barranco* into a field and continue on the lower path to pass below a small stone cabin/corral and above a ruin.

The path then starts winding down towards the river. You'll soon see a stand of poplars downriver and beyond them the path climbing to **Capileira** from **Puente Buchite**, which we reach in thirty minutes from Wp.8. Once over the bridge, a scramble across rocks on the left leads into a lovely picnic spot on the riverbank underneath the poplars.

The final climb to **Capileira** follows the stony path up from the bridge, soon passing a waypost (Wp.9) marking a branch down to **Puente Chiscar**. We continue on the main path to join the dirt track into **Capileira**, arriving at the **Mirador de Aldeire** threshing circles (Wp.10 145M) after a twenty-five minute climb from the river.

Mirador de Aldeire

We then follow the paved track, the **Paseo de Aldeire**, into **Capileira**. The alley on the left just before the **Apartamentos Vista Veleta** leads back to the start of the walk, while **Calle del Cubo** in front of the *Apartamentos* brings us up to **Plaza Calvario** and the **Bar El Tilo**.

18 RÍO NAUTE CIRCUIT

This is an exceptional itinerary, along with **El Caballo** our favourite high-mountain route, a walk of delicate beauty and sublime grandeur, climbing from **La Cebadilla** through land that gets ever wilder with fabulous views before descending from the **Cámara de Carga** along the *tubería*, the waterpipe feeding the 'Central Poqueira' turbines. What's more, if you're lucky, you may meet Paco 'El Pastor Poeta', 'the Shepherd Poet', who spends his summers at the **Cortijo Toril** with his brother, and is only too happy to regale passers-by with recitals of his poems lamenting the many women who have failed to love him as he would have wished. Access via **Pista Forestal 3**: turn left at km 2.7 and follow the dirt track down to **Puente Hondera**. If the space is free, park in the shade of the cliffs just west of the *puente*. The walk starts as per the newly designated **PR23**.

The power station

Short Version
Turn back at the bridge over the **Río Veleta (Wp.8)** 2½ hours return.

From **Puente Hondera** (Wp.1 0M), we take the concrete track up to the power station and cross the bridges over the **Ríos Toril** and **Naute** to a mapboard outlining a version of this walk. We then cross the concrete ledge after the mapboard and take the mule trail climbing away from the **Río Naute**.

Ignoring a minor branch on the right five minutes later, we continue climbing using the shortcuts according to taste, haste and lung capacity. One shortcut (emerging at a triangulation post, Wp.2 20M) has virtually replaced the original route. After a series of zigzags and a long steady climb, the trail levels out just before a branch to the left (Wp.3 25M) climbs to **Puente Toril** (Wp.17), our return route.

We continue on the main, level trail, as it dwindles to a dirt path passing a *cortijo*/byre before climbing gently to a second, ruined *cortijo* (**Cortijo Masagrande**, Wp.4 35M) beside two wayposts, one indicating another path up to **Puente Toril**. We stay on the main path as it descends very slightly to pass immediately behind a white-painted *cortijo*, after which another gentle climb leads up to two large walnut trees, and a wayposted path down towards the river and the **Cortijo de la Isla**, visible on a small rise in the middle of the river.

Bearing left at the top of a rough, boulder-strewn spur, we follow the clear but eroded path down to the rocky right bank of the **Río Naute**. Two small bridges fifty metres below the **Cortijo de la Isla** cross the watercourses defining the island before a third bridge brings us to the *cortijo* itself (Wp.5 55M), where the landscape becomes much wilder and greener. We then follow the path up **La Isla** behind the *cortijo* towards the escarpment of the **Tajo Cañavate**, bearing right after a few minutes to climb over a knoll to another waypost (Wp.6 60M). Another rough bridge crosses the lower reaches of the **Barranco de Cañavate** and, a hundred metres later, yet another bridge leads into a marshy green meadow on the right bank of the main river.

The path gets narrower here and is occasionally waterlogged as it climbs past another ruin, before bearing away from the river into a steeper climb. We zigzag up a rock-laid stretch, ignoring a branch on the right to join a gentler gradient leading to a Y-junction (Wp.7 80M).

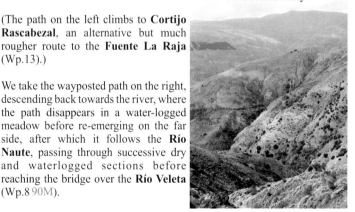

Río Naute valley

(The path on the left climbs to **Cortijo Rascabezal**, an alternative but much rougher route to the **Fuente La Raja** (Wp.13).)

We take the wayposted path on the right, descending back towards the river, where the path disappears in a water-logged meadow before re-emerging on the far side, after which it follows the **Río Naute**, passing through successive dry and waterlogged sections before reaching the bridge over the **Río Veleta** (Wp.8 90M).

Beyond the bridge a very narrow path climbs through dense vegetation, briefly following the left bank of the **Río Veleta** before veering back towards the **Naute**. The landscape becomes wilder and drier as the path climbs past occasional cairns before circling a large rocky outcrop to another junction (Wp.9 105M) marked by two wayposts.

The main path on the right leads up to **Cortijo Las Tomas** and the **Poqueira Refuge** (see Walk 21) both of which have been clearly visible for much of the preceding hour. We, however, turn left onto a rough narrow path climbing the rise between the **Ríos Veleta** and **Naute**.

The path climbs steeply, occasionally losing definition, but the route is clearly marked by cairns and concrete triangulation posts. To the left, you'll soon see the concrete installations at **Fuente La Raja** (Wp.13), our next objective. Bearing left at the remains of a threshing circle (Wp.10 125M), we follow the cairns till the path bears right at a waypost (Wp.11 127M) where we leave the waymarked route to take a shortcut.

N.B. The 'official' route is almost as wild as the shortcut, but if you're doing this in reverse, stick to the official route as it's better marked with cairns.

We bear left at Wp.11 and, fifty metres after the waypost, start climbing a shaley slope past the remains of ramparts that once shored up a path, heading for a sharp rock tipped with a concrete triangulation post. Bearing left ten metres below the triangulation post, we continue climbing towards a large cairn on a rock below the cliffs (Wp.12 140M) where we rejoin the sketchily waymarked route along a rough path below the cliffs. This path follows the underground pipe taking water from the **Río Naute** to the **Fuente La Raja**, **La Cámara de Carga** and, eventually, the **Central de Poqueira**.

Ramal del Naute (as seen from the south-east)

As you follow this path, you may care to glance across to the far bank of the **Río Veleta**. A little way above the clear green line of an open *acequia*, you should be able to make out the continuation of the underground pipe from **Fuente La Raja**, the **Ramal del Naute**.

Despite the daunting looking pinnacle of rock rising above it (the 2177 metre height point on our map), this marks our route. The faint path climbing behind the pinnacle is where we're heading and it's nothing like as horrifying as it looks from a distance. Promise!

Just after the installations at **Fuente La Raja** (a gloriously wild place despite all the concrete) the path divides in front of a tiny hut with a faded green door (Wp.13 155M). Ignore the branch descending on the left to the *acequia* and follow the underground pipe for a hundred metres to an inspection hatch (a stone tower with a concrete lid), ten metres after which, we bear right onto a very rough path marked with cairns that climbs for five minutes to a pass behind the pinnacles.

At first, the path beyond the pinnacles is indistinct, but if you pick your way down the slope for ten metres, you'll soon recover a clear if rough path that passes above a stone water hut. After a brief climb behind the water hut, the path becomes smoother and another gentle climb leads up to a waypost

(Wp.14 180M) where it's worth pausing to look back at the distinctive peak of **Veleta**.

Cámara de Carga

The path then bears round the mountain before descending back to the **Ramal del Naute** waterpipe at an inspection hatch five minutes from Wp.14 (Wp.15 if you're doing this route in reverse) from where it's easy, level walking all the way to the **Cámara de Carga** and its *tubería*, the unmistakable silver pipe descending to **La Cebadilla**.

The tracks splinter as you near the **Cámara de Carga**. You can either take the shortcut, the first branch on the left, or continue till two cairns (Wp.16 200M), fifty metres from the **Cámara** fence, indicate the main route down to the eastern side of the *tubería*. The path descends parallel to the *tubería*, gradually broadening and tracing long loops to break the descent, before coming directly alongside it and running into a slightly steeper descent down to a well-built wooden bridge, the **Puente Toril** (Wp.17 225M), which crosses the *tubería* to join the path to the *cortijos* along the **Río Toril**.

Our path meanwhile bears left at the bridge and zigzags down to a small outcrop of rock tipped with stubby holm oak. We bear right at a large cairn and take the rough but clear path to the right of the outcrop, descending to Wp.3 from where we follow the outward route back to **La Cebadilla** in a little under half-an-hour.

Along with the **Naute**, the **Río Toril** forms the last fork in the feed streams that form the **Río Poqueira**, and as such is one of the Alpujarras' most important water sources. It's a wonderful wild little valley with few trees and a wide open high mountain feel to it, and its *acequias* (the **Amoladeras**, **Sevillana**, **Nueva**, and **Castillejos**) are a delight.

The classic tour is a loop via Puente **Toril** (see Walk 18) and the **Acequia Nueva**, but a landslip above the *cortijos* on the river's northern bank makes that outing a little heavy going. The present itinerary is, in its way, no less arduous, since it involves a long central climb off path on rough ground, but walking two *acequias* in one itinerary (the **Nueva** and the **Castillejos**) is such a glorious indulgence the exertion and pathfinding challenges are amply recompensed. Access via **Pista Forestal 3**: turn left at km2.7 and follow the dirt track down to **Puente Hondero**. If the space is free, park in the shade of the cliffs on the right bank of the river. Otherwise there's plenty of room beside the bricked up chapel 100 metres before the bridge.

Access: by car or on foot from **Capileira** (see Walk 17)

Short Versions
(a) turn left at Wp.5 to pick up the return at Wp.12
(b) stay on the **Acequia Nueva** after Wp.7 till it ends in the riverbed then return the same way

Starting from **Puente Hondero** (Wp.1 0M), we take the dirt track for 'Puente Abuchite'. After a steady climb, the wayposted path to **Capileira** forks left (Wp.2 9M), but we stay on the track, climbing steadily to steeply to a second wayposted path, this time doubling back to the right, at which point we leave the dirt track (Wp.3 23M).

The Río Toril Valley

Our stony path zigzags up between stumpy oaks, passing a succession of crumbling ruins and a faint branch path doubling back to the left (Wp.4 35M). Eventually, we climb above the main growth of wood, fine views of **Mulhacén** and the **Cebadilla** *tubería* (see walks 22 & 18) opening out on our right. The gradient gradually eases as we approach then join the **Acequia Nueva** (Wp.5 45M), where we bear right and begin a delightful stroll along the level *acequia* path into the **Río Toril** valley.

There's no call for talk here, just walk and enjoy, however if you intend doing the full walk, it's worth noting that the patch

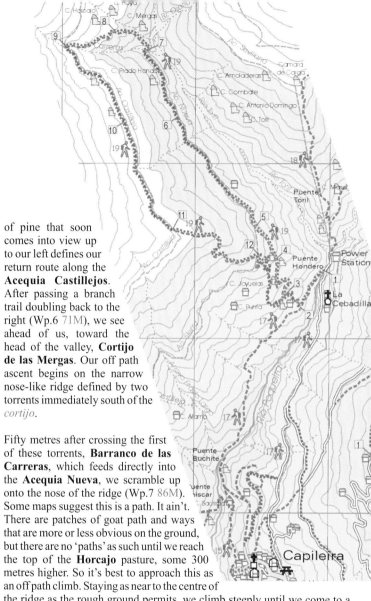

of pine that soon comes into view up to our left defines our return route along the **Acequia Castillejos**. After passing a branch trail doubling back to the right (Wp.6 71M), we see ahead of us, toward the head of the valley, **Cortijo de las Mergas**. Our off path ascent begins on the narrow nose-like ridge defined by two torrents immediately south of the *cortijo*.

Fifty metres after crossing the first of these torrents, **Barranco de las Carreras**, which feeds directly into the **Acequia Nueva**, we scramble up onto the nose of the ridge (Wp.7 86M). Some maps suggest this is a path. It ain't. There are patches of goat path and ways that are more or less obvious on the ground, but there are no 'paths' as such until we reach the top of the **Horcajo** pasture, some 300 metres higher. So it's best to approach this as an off path climb. Staying as near to the centre of the ridge as the rough ground permits, we climb steeply until we come to a tiny, grassy *acequia*, from where the line of the **Acequia Castillejos** is already visible as it cuts away from the top of the **Barranco de las Carreras** toward a small *cortijo* off to our left (Wp.8 107M).

Following the mini-*acequia* round to the west, we cross its feed spring then scramble (still very much off path) onto the foot of the **Horcajo** grazing ground, a high, ragged pasture splashed with patches of bracken. Maintaining a westerly direction, taking advantage of the occasional tiny patches of cow path, and climbing whenever compelled by one of the swales feeding the **Carreras** torrent, we contour round the **Horcajo** pasture. There's no one way here, but as a rough guide we stay between the 2140-2175 metre mark, until we reach the canalization point at the intersection of **Barranco de las Carreras** and **Acequia Castillejos**, the line of which is visible throughout our traverse of the pasture (Wp.9 122M). Relax, the rough bit's done and we're back to pure pleasure again!

After that stiff little scramble across the pasture, the way south along the *acequia* and past the *cortijo* seen from below is a blast and the only advice I can give is not to stride out too fast and miss the magnificent views. We draw abreast of the pine wood more or less at the halfway mark of our stroll along the *acequia* (Wp.10 137M). Shortly after crossing a gully of grey shale and just before the *acequia* swings southwest, we fork left on a clear but <u>unmarked</u> path (Wp.11 152M).

The path descends to the southeast, gently at first then more steeply as the **Poqueira** villages come into view off to our right.

Acequia Nueva

After passing a solitary boulder, our way veers south toward the top of the oak wood, then resumes an easterly direction, rejoining the **Acequia Nueva** just south of Wp.5 (Wp.12 170M). Crossing the *acequia*, we join the end of the track climbing from **La Cebadilla**, which we follow down to rejoin our outward route at Wp.3 (185M).

Although the climb is not huge and the terrain is not particularly difficult, this can seem like an unusually tough walk, perhaps because there's plenty of opportunity for getting lost, so you need good pathfinding skills. For the rambler, the main attractions are the magnificent views, but there's also the added interest of visiting the Buddhist centre, built in honour of Osel Hita, the first westerner recognised as a reincarnated lama. The centre is open to visitors between 3 & 6 p.m. Our itinerary does not actually 'visit' **O.Sel.Ling**, but given that this is a spiritual retreat, I suggest timing the walk to cross the premises during official visiting hours. Presumably if you're contemplating the divine, you don't necessarily welcome a bunch of big-booted ramblers blundering through your meditations.

** but given the pathfinding problems allow 6 hours walking time.

* in **Bubíon**, though you might get a free cup of tea from the students on residential courses if you're lucky.

From **Plaza de la Iglesia** in **Bubíon**, we take the **Calle Real**, then the concrete lane (**Calle Liso**) and the paved lane down to the cross at the corner of the football field (0M), from where we can see, on the tip of **Atalaya** (Wp.14) to the SW, the tiny white speck of the firewatch hut above **O.Sel.Ling**.

Short Version

To avoid 90% of the climb, drive to the centre and start from there, or from Wp.17. Take **Pista Forestal 2** and turn right onto the **O-Sel.Ling** branch setting the odometer at zero. At km2.3, go left for **O.Sel.Ling** or right for the track below Wp.17, after which km3.5=Wp.18, km4.8=Wp.20, and km5.6=Wp.10. Follow the walk as described but stay on the dirt track at Wp.20 till Wp.10 (3 walker, 2½ hours).

The 2.3km branch on the stroll

We then take the broad path below the football field, passing the **Barrancos de Tejar** (aka **Alguastar**) and **Armuña** before descending to the **Puente Molino** (Wp.1 24M). Crossing the river, we climb to a junction (Wp.2 31M), where we turn right and head north to be greeted by smiles and barks (see Walk 15) at the **Cortijo Enrique** (Wp.3 40M).

Bearing left between the main building and a woodshed, we climb past a ruin and a threshing circle to join another path (Wp.4 51M), where we bear right, crossing the **Barranco de las Rosas** to another junction (Wp.5 62M). We then turn left on the orange and turquoise waymarked path and climb back towards the centre of the *barranco* to a small stone and concrete bridge (Wp.6 70M).

After another steepish ascent, we leave the waymarked path as it bears left and take the unmarked path on the right to climb above the *barranco* towards a tall, half dead chestnut tree. Just behind some ruins and a small mulberry tree (Wp.7 79M) the path swings right onto a steep, water-eroded slope where it splits into several goat tracks threading through a wall of *retama*.

We stick to the main track, along which a small scarlet stripe painted on a rock (Wp.8 86M) suggests this is an official route, appearances notwithstanding. Following the main traces, we scramble up a steep scree slope until it emerges onto a flat area (Wp.9 99M) to the right of a dry watercourse and dirt track. There's also a small red dot on a rock to our right and a line of embedded stones forming a channel in the slope ahead.

Bearing left across the dry watercourse, we ignore the grassy track climbing into a field and follow the lower dirt track to pass behind a *cortijo* at the back of which there are four columns topped with orange iron bars. One hundred and fifty metres later we pass below the more substantial **Cortijo Bañuelo** (black metal gates and balustrades, and a magnificent walnut tree). If you glance up just after the **Cortijo Bañuelo**, you'll see a ruined cabin (Wp.11) three hundred metres above. This is our next objective.

N.B. If the **Cortijo Bañuelo** happens to be unoccupied, immediately after the *cortijo* with columns you can take the driveway up to the **Bañuelo** walnut tree and climb directly behind the *cortijo*.

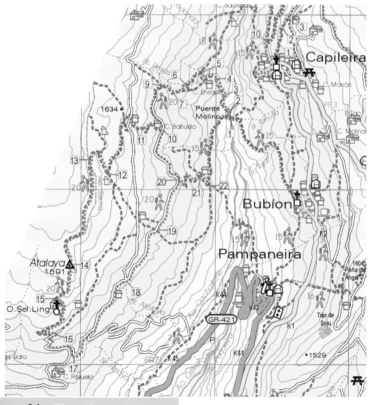

Otherwise, seventy-five metres past **Bañuelo**, a faint path (Wp.10 110M) climbs between an eglantine bush and brambles under a smaller walnut tree.

*If you're coming from the south on the short version, **Cortijo Bañuelo** is the *cortijo* with a solar panel mounted in one corner, one hundred and fifty metres after a line of tin baths in the field on your right.

There's no single path up to the ruin, which disappears briefly as we start climbing, but about halfway between **Bañuelo** and the ruin (visible again), just above the fourth terrace behind the *cortijo*, something akin to a path crosses two more terraces (SW) before switching back via a long-abandoned water reservoir to climb to the ruin (Wp.11 124M).

After circling another ancient reservoir behind the ruin, we take a narrow path up to a forestry track twenty metres above the ruin. We turn right on this track, then bear left when another track comes in from the right. You can relax now. Most of the pathfinding problems are past!

Fine views into the Poqueira Gorge

Climbing steadily but gently with splendid views over the **Poqueira Gorge** and the **Sierras Lújar** and **Contraviessa**, the track passes a house (Wp.12 137M) on our left and a branch on our right before crossing the **Acequia Nueva** (Wp.13 151M).

Ten metres after the *acequia* we leave the main track and take the branch to the left. We follow this branch track as it bears round the mountain and turns into a firebreak then turn left onto another dirt track down to the white-roofed firewatch hut, just beyond the concrete triangulation point marking the **Atalaya** (Wp.14 160M).

We then follow the dirt track past the firewatch hut and, when it bears right (W), maintain direction (S) to a white-painted concrete post, on the right of which a stony path descends towards (SW) a long narrow white flag. If the flag's not flying, aim for a large field with a small stand of oak slightly off-centre and, at its SE end, an outcrop of rock where the flag normally is. Ten metres later, and one hundred metres short of the flag, the stony path joins a clearer, grassy path (Wp.15 174M) just above a water-tank with a round metal manhole cover circled in white.

Following the grassy path past the water tank, we pass between the uppermost **O.Sel.Ling** buildings (accommodation for those attending residential courses) onto a dirt track. Following the dirt track down past the showers (water sometimes available) and the camping area, we soon see the 'stupa' (a symbol; Buddha's mind, which apparently resembled a wedding cake) and the coppery roof of a shrine.

Looking south from below O.Sel.Ling

At the car-park beside the main entrance (Wp.16 180M), we bear right and follow the dirt track down till a cairn (Wp.17 204M) on the left marks a clear path crossing a patch of grass peppered with goat pellets to a large holm oak twenty metres away, where the path drops onto another dirt track and we bear left.

Ignoring the first two branches on the right, we follow the main track which climbs gradually before passing behind a large byre. The gradient gets slightly steeper then eases off again alongside older cabins and byres. Thirty metres after a large oak on the right, we bear right on another dirt track (Wp.18 219M) with a very faint red paintmark on a rock on the left after four metres.

We then follow this track as it climbs very slightly, passing a branch on the right forty metres later and another on the left (Wp.19 230M) that climbs to a white-painted house in the distance. Ignoring a second track up to the white-painted house, we follow the main track as it descends past a recently fenced field.

Eventually, the track curves round another broader flatter field running up to a ruin; just as it starts to climb again, we turn right on another track (too rough to be a *pista forestal*, too broad to be a path) (Wp.20 242M) and descend (SE) towards some oak trees. There's also a tiny red dot two metres down this track.

One hundred and fifty metres later this rough track bears sharp left and then winds down above a stone cabin, where it dwindles to a path. To the north of the cabin, a narrow path (Wp.21 256M) comes in from our left. DO NOT take this path. If you do you may well end up on **Pico de Alegas**!

We stay on the same path we've descended as it bears round below the cabin and continues descending to a small ruined *cortijo*. 5 metres after the ruin, we bear left onto a path (Wp.22 259M) crossing the grassy area below. After the grassy area, the path crosses a small oak wood and three watercourses (the first two usually dry) before making its definitive steep descent to **Puente Molino**, fifteen minutes from the ruin and thirty minutes from **Bubíon**.

A glorious, easily accessible high-mountain walk taking one of the traditional routes to visit the impressive **Poqueira Refuge** and returning by one of two lovely *acequia* paths. If you want to have lunch at the refuge, make sure you arrive before 3 p.m. as the kitchen is closed between 3 and 5.30 p.m.

* to **Poqueira Refuge** 4/5
to **Cortijo de las Tomas** 2

** to **Cortijo de las Tomas** 1 hour 50 mins (one-way)
to **Cortijo de las Tomas**, returning by the *acequia* 4 hours
to **Poqueira Refuge** 2¾ hours (one-way)

*** at the **Poqueira Refuge**

Access by car: To reach the start of the walk, take the **Hoya del Portillo** road from **Capileira** (**Pista Forestal 3**), setting your odometer at zero when you leave the tarmac. At km2 the road bears sharp right and we turn left onto a dirt track just after a nicely restored *cortijo*. Eight hundred metres along the track, park at the triangular chimney wall of an unfinished house just before the **Acequia Baja** (Wp.1). If you don't have a car, you can ask the Parque Natural bus from **Capileira** to drop you off at the 2km turning. If you're walking in winter and there's a risk of snow, park at the end of the tarmac.

Short Versions
(1) Return from **Cortijo de Las Tomas** without climbing to the refuge (see text).

(2) Take the dirt track or the *acequia* back from **Corrales de Pitres**.

Acequia Baja

One hundred metres after crossing the **Acequia Baja** we turn left on another dirt track (usually chained off) which soon brings us in sight of the **Poqueira Refuge** below the **Mulhacén**. A little under one kilometre from the chimney, the track goes through a sharp right-hand bend then swings back north. Just before it bears right again, we take the faint path (Wp.2 15M) on the left below some rocks.

The path soon becomes clear, winding along the contour lines and crossing a series of watercourses until it joins a broader, waymarked path (Wp.3 40M) climbing from **Capileira** (an alternative return route if you came by bus, though bear in mind it's a 600 metre descent from here to **Capileira**).

After crossing a torrent a few minutes later, we continue along the waymarked path to the goat pens at the **Corrales de Pitres** (Wp.4 55M) where the dirt track we left at Wp.2 ends and a lot of barking begins. Passing below the stone cabins and ignoring the track climbing to the right, we follow the waymarked path to the left, after which you can see in a direct line below the refuge, the **Cortijo de Las Tomas**, our next objective.

The path joins the **Acequia Alta** (Wp.5 65M) beside two wayposts, but bears away from it one hundred metres later for a descent that gives fine views of the **Picos de Pulpito** and **Sabinar**, which when seen from further away tend to be swallowed up by the higher peaks behind them.

After passing a ruined stone corral with two wayposts in front of it, we follow the main path and descend to cross a meagre torrent. The path climbs to run alongside a narrow *acequia* for a few metres before descending past two more wayposts and crossing another torrent, eventually climbing slightly to the **Cortijo de las Tomas** (Wp.6 110M) from where there are magnificent views down the gorge towards the **Sierra Lújar**.

So far we've only climbed about one hundred metres. If you don't fancy the steep climb to the refuge (400 metres straight up) you could opt for the alternative ending here. Otherwise, to climb to the refuge, we take the signposted path behind the *cortijo* (NE). After trudging up the first couple of hundred metres, we hop over the **Acequia Alta** (Wp.7 120M) and continue trudging (there's no other word for it).

The refuge is, distressingly, out of sight, but the path is clear and well-marked with cairns, so there are no path-finding problems and you can concentrate on your trudging.

After a little over thirty minutes of remorseless trudging, we bear left to cross a marshy area and follow the path winding up through a rocky area dotted with so many cairns it looks like the site of a lunar cult. The object here is to cross the north-west tip of the rocky ridge that has loomed above us throughout our trudge. Beyond the ridge a waypost marks the last thankfully gentle climb to the refuge (Wp.8 165M), where somebody has thoughtfully built a cement climbing wall on the porch!

Approaching the refuge

The **Poqueira Refuge** (Tel: 958 343 349) is well worth the trudge. It's solidly built, magnificently appointed, immaculately kept, and has excellent dormitory facilities, hot showers, a self-access kitchen, and a complete bar and restaurant service - and you need restoring after your trudge.

The Poqueira Refuge

It's also a good place to stay a few nights for exploring the higher peaks. The guides running the refuge can give you the appropriate information. If you want to stay over, they do have blankets and sell disposable sheets, but it's best if you bring your own sleeping bag.

We now retrace our steps to Wp.7, where we have a choice of return routes, one via the **Acequia Alta**, the other via the **Acequia Baja**. The option you choose largely depends on which has water in it, as an *acequia* without water loses nine tenths of its charm. As a general rule, the **Acequia Baja** always has water and the views are, possibly, a little better. If both have water, the **Acequia Baja** is the better option as it's more likely to have water till the end. There are, however, one or two stretches on this option that are very, very mildly vertiginous. In both cases, the path is rough and occasionally narrow, so you have to watch where you're putting your feet and stop to admire the splendid views.

Option A Acequia Alta
It's hard to get lost following an *acequia*, but note the following Waypoints:
(Wp.9 240M) we briefly rejoin the outward path (see Wp.5).
(Wp.10 250M) we cross the dirt track above the **Corrales de Pitres**, after which an overgrowth of eglantine obliges us to drop down occasionally on goat tracks. Beware of irrigation gates concealed by marsh grass.
(Wp.11 290M) we rejoin the **Corrales de Pitres** dirt track two minutes above Wp.2, 20 minutes from Wp.1.

Option B Acequia Baja
Descend to Wp.6 and continue descending past **Cortijo de las Tomas**, off path for 100 metres, down to the **Acequia Baja** (Wp.12 202M). We hop over the watercourse onto the *acequero*'s path, turn left and off we go. Once again, there's no call for description, but for the purposes of pacing progress:
(Wp.13 221M) the *acequia* passes between a fissured rock obliging us to drop down below it very briefly;
(Wp.14 237M) we cross **Barranco Cañavate**
(Wp.15 266M) after traversing a gaping scar of shale, two makeshift bridges take us onto the left bank of the *acequia* to avoid damaging the narrow outer wall;
(Wp.16 276M) we cross the wayposted path descending on the right to **Capileira**, after which we simply continue along the *acequia*, traversing the band of pine visible ahead to return to Wp.1.

Veleta and Mulhacén, seen from Loma de Cáñar

The **Mulhacén** is the highest mountain on the Iberian Peninsula and therefore a must for many visitors. This circuit is intermittently waymarked and poses no serious orientation problems. It's not the most interesting ascent, but it is the most practical day trip. For the most part it's an easy walk along clear dirt tracks, however it is very, very long and the final climb to the peak is very steep. The park leaflet claims it takes seven hours, I timed it at eight-and-a-half, but given the length and height climbed, you should allow up to twelve hours counting rest-stops.

This route is included as the most practical single-day circuit to the top. But the descent is a bit boring! If you have the option of being picked up at the end of the day and have good pathfinding skills, or have already done Walks 18 & 21, I recommend taking the bus from **Capileira** to the **Mirador de Trevélez**, following either of the Short Versions to the top, then descending via the **Caldera** and **Poqueira** refuges and the **Río Naute** to **La Cebadilla**. Beware though: the link path crossing the headwaters of the **Naute from Cortijo de las Tomas** is a little vertiginous and involves crawling on hands and knees for a couple of metres.

If you walk the route in winter
The **Mulhacén** can be climbed in winter, particularly in February when the weather tends to be more stable, but given the steepness of its western face, I'd recommend using our descent route as the ascent and coming back the same way. Length might also dictate an overnight stay at the **Poqueira Refuge**. Snow may make the **Hoya del Portillo** start inaccessible as late as Easter, in which case you could park at the firebreak at km8.9 on **PF3** and start climbing from there to pick up the described walk at Wp.3.

Walking the route in summer
In summer, late July, early August are the best times, before the electric storms begin. The most likely problem you'll have with the weather is wind, though snow can stay on the peak as late as August. The problem with a summer ascent is that, by the time you get to the top, heat will have hazed the views for which the peak is so justly renowned. The only way round this is to camp out at the **Refuge Caldera** and climb early in the morning. Summer temperatures

are pleasant at this altitude, but the UV is very intense: sun-hat, sunglasses, sun-cream are ESSENTIAL; long sleeves/trousers recommended. Water is available at the **Refuge Poqueira**, but has such a vile taste it's best to bring your own.

Several dirt tracks are used here. I use the local name for the main one, the **Carretera de Veleta** (**PF3** after the chain).

The short version (see below) from the **Mirador de Trevélez/Alto de Chorillo** is only possible in summer, when the park authority bus drops ramblers off in the morning and picks them up in the evening. Enquire at the Information Office in **Capileira**. **Hoya del Portillo** is the point to which private cars are allowed. Only the early and late buses go to the **Mirador de Trevélez**. However, all buses go to the new *mirador* at **Puerto Molina**. Book the **Mirador de Trevélez** bus in advance (Tel: 686 414 576); at the height of the season it can be booked up for several days ahead.

* 5+ for the full walk, though to be honest, length and altitude send it off the scale. It's not difficult but you need a lot of stamina.

** Given the sheer length of this walk, I've broken times up for easier reference:
Hoya del Portillo - Poqueira Refuge 2 hours 10 mins
Poqueira Refuge - Caldera Refuge 2 hours 10 mins
Caldera Refuge - Mulhacén 1 hour 10 mins
Mulhacén - Hoya del Portillo 3 hours 5 mins

*** at the **Poqueira Refuge** - a lower rating than in Walk 21 as it comes too soon in this itinerary to be really useful.

	Strolls
Buses back: see the Short Version.	(a) **Hoya del Portillo** pine forest - follow the main walk to **Puerto de Molina** (Wp.3) and return via the **Carretera de Veleta** (b) **Puerto de Molina** - **Loma de Piedra Blanca**. Take the bus to **Puerto Molina** and, starting on the faint path behind the *mirador*, follow the ridge (NE) for twenty-five minutes to **Prado Llano**, distinguished by a concrete triangulation post and stunning views. Head east along faint tractor-tracks to take the **Carretera de Veleta** back to **Puerto Molina**.

HOYA DEL PORTILLO - POQUEIRA REFUGE (2 hours 10 minutes)
From the barrier at the end of **Pista Forestal 3** (Wp.1 0M), we take the path to the left of the control hut up to the Gaudi-like grottoes and information centre. On the right of the white-painted building, we take the wayposted path up through the pine forest to a firebreak (Wp.2 25M). We then follow this path until it turns left and crosses the firebreak at **Puerto Molina** (Wp.3 30M) between two small wayposts and two tall (currently 'signless') signposts. We cross the firebreak and take the broad dirt track west.

The track descends slightly before bearing right and levelling out. Ignoring a minor branch on the left (Wp.4 50M), we stick to the main track climbing gently towards the **Cascar Negro** quarries. At the first quarry, when the track bears right, we turn left onto a broad, wayposted path (Wp.5 60M) that soon widens to a dirt track climbing past another extraction site.

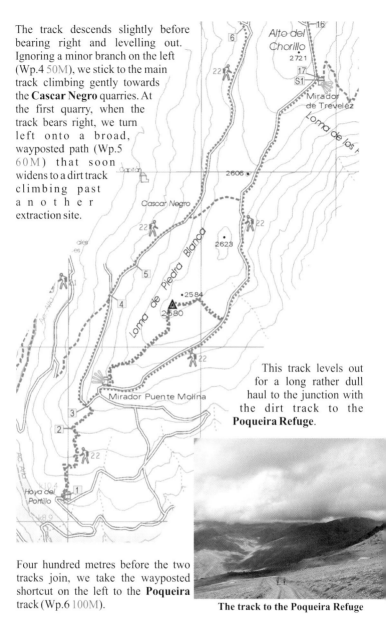

This track levels out for a long rather dull haul to the junction with the dirt track to the **Poqueira Refuge**.

Four hundred metres before the two tracks join, we take the wayposted shortcut on the left to the **Poqueira** track (Wp.6 100M).

The track to the Poqueira Refuge

We bear left on this track then right behind the rocky outcrop and stone byre to descend to the **Poqueira Refuge** (Wp.7 130M).

POQUEIRA REFUGE - CALDERA REFUGE (2 hours 10 minutes)

Taking the well-trodden path from the refuge (NW), we gradually bear right (N) to join the **Río Mulhacén** ten minutes later. We then follow the left bank of the river (N) till the river runs dry, where we cross onto the right bank beside a cairn (Wp.8 35M).

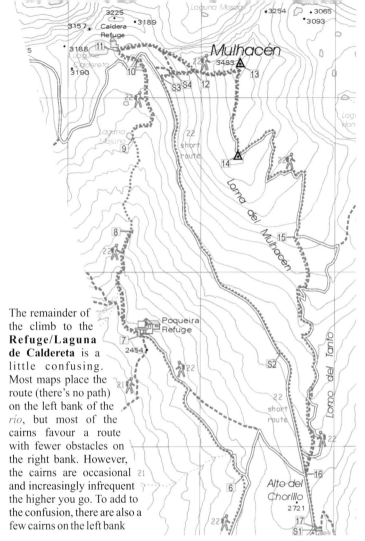

The remainder of the climb to the **Refuge/Laguna de Caldereta** is a little confusing. Most maps place the route (there's no path) on the left bank of the *río*, but most of the cairns favour a route with fewer obstacles on the right bank. However, the cairns are occasional and increasingly infrequent the higher you go. To add to the confusion, there are also a few cairns on the left bank

Nonetheless, if you keep climbing north, insofar as obstacles allow, you can't go far wrong. The route described here is the one on the right bank, bearing away from the river to avoid the steeper, rougher stretches. The walking is easier, but the pathfinding is harder. If you're doing the itinerary in reverse, it's best to follow the course of the river where the cairns are better placed for those approaching from above.

A steady climb following the cairns (NNE) comes out a little to the east of the **Laguna Majuno** (Wp.9 90M). After bearing right alongside the marshy area feeding the lagoon, we climb a shallow stony depression (N) between a rocky outcrop and the **Carretera de Veleta**, which is clearly visible 100 metres above.

This depression leads into a grassy swale which we follow towards the centre of the *cirque* defined by the **Mulhacén** and the **Puntal de la Caldera**, crossing another (probably dry) lagoon onto the *carretera* (Wp.10 125M). Crossing the *carretera*, we maintain direction to reach the unmanned but well-maintained **Caldera Refuge** (Wp.11 130M) overlooking the lagoon.

CALDERA REFUGE - MULHACÉN (1 hour 10 minutes)

East of the refuge, the main path up to the peak is clearly visible. About halfway up, another narrower path comes in from the left. This is the path to take for a slightly gentler start to the ascent.

Following the faint path east from the refuge, we cross a brief pathless stretch over rocks before recovering the trodden way above the splendid jagged cliffs on the northern face of the **Mulhacén**.

After the two paths join (Wp.12 30M), comes the really testing bit - straight up through the most modestly sketched zigzags to the peak (Wp.13 70M), which will probably be relatively crowded, both with Spanish hikers (who are always ready to share their expertise on their favourite local mountains) and *cabra montés* so blasé about human beings, they're almost domestic.

On a clear day, you can see as far as Algeria (the ruins on the top are left over from a geodesic triangulation survey of North Africa at the end of the nineteenth century) though the likelihood is, you'll not see much further than a great expanse of white to the south-east, the *Mar de Plastico* or 'Plastic Sea', covering the Dalías Plain near Almería and responsible for all those chemical tomatoes littering supermarket shelves in England in the winter. However, even on the haziest of days, the views are breathtaking and there's a certain dizzying pleasure to be had from peering over the cliffs to the north, down to the **Laguna de la Mosca**, 500 metres below, a climb some demented enthusiasts undertake in winter when it's a wall of ice - not always with ropes either!

MULHACÉN - HOYA DEL PORTILLO (3 hours 5 minutes)

The descent is easy, but dull and very, very long. We start along the ridge to the south, along a clearly trodden path that soon joins a stony dirt track laid at the time of geodesic survey and currently neatly covered with blocks of rock in an attempt to regenerate the natural landscape. The track bears left just before a cluster of rock-shelters/windbreaks and another triangulation post (Wp.14 15M) sometimes known as **Mulhacén II**, from where we have clear views of the way back to the **Hoya del Portillo**.

Whether you follow the track all the way down to **Alto de Chorillo** or take the shortcuts (notably Wp.15 45M marked by a cairn), is a matter for you and your knees to come to an arrangement over, but as a general rule, the lower we go the easier and more inevitable the shortcuts seem. Taking the shortcuts, we join the **Carretera de Veleta** a few hundred metres south of the end of the track from **Mulhacén**.

We then follow the *carretera* south, passing the junction with the **Poqueira** track and signs saying 'El Chorillo' (Wp.16 95M) and the 'Mirador de Trevélez' (Wp.17 105M) where the bus stops.

We then continue along the *carretera* past the small peaks of the **Loma de Piedra Blanca** (it takes 'forever', in reality a little under an hour) until it eventually goes through a U-bend round the new *mirador* below which we leave the *carretera* and take the firebreak down to **Puerto Molina** and the path (Wp.3) through the pine forest to **Hoya del Portillo** (185M).

Short Version
(via the **Loma de Mulhacén**: 4 walker, 4 hours; via **Caldera**: 5 walker, 4 hours)

Take the eight o'clock bus from **Capileira** to the **Mirador de Trevélez/Alto de Chorillo** (WpS.1 0M), follow the **Carretera de Veleta** (NNW), ignoring branches to left (**Poqueira Refuge**) and right (**Loma de Mulhacén**) before passing a second red-and-white barrier (WpS.2 25M). A few-hundred metres before the **Caldera Refuge**, take the clearly trodden path on the right (WpS.3 75M) up to join first the main path from the *carretera* (WpS.4 83M) then the minor path from **Caldera** (Wp.12).

If the **Mulhacén** is still under snow, take the **Loma de Mulhacén** branch of the track for both the ascent and descent.

Pórtugos - AR Río Bermejo - (ext. Haza del Cerezo) - Capilerilla - Pórtugos

A pleasant walk through the oak forest above the **Tahá** climbing to an exceptional site, the dramatic cleft in the rock where the **Barrancos del Chorrera** and **Jabalí** converge to form the **Río Bermejo** - take your towel. If you don't like pathless slopes and unstable footing, ignore the extension. Either park in **Pórtugos**, at the western end of **Plaza de la Iglesia** or in the **Plaza Nueva**, or where the walk actually starts, at the top of the concrete track climbing from the petrol station.

* 3 with the extension ** +30 minutes for the extension *** in **Pórtugos**

From the **Plaza de la Iglesia** in **Pórtugos**, we take **Calle Abulagillas** next to the **Productos Carnicos Moises**, then turn right to pass the **Jamones Casa Juan** and cross **Plaza de Churriana**, leaving the village via **Calle Rosario**, which bears right off **Calle Churriana**.

Once out of the village, we follow the track to the white cross (0M), one hundred metres after which we bear right up a partially concreted track. We follow this track, ignoring all branches until, fifty metres after the second stretch of concrete, the main track bears sharp right and we take the branch on the left. Since several 'tracks' appear in the next few minutes, I'll call this branch the *pista forestal*.

When the *pista forestal* crosses an *acequia* below a large, cement walled house (Wp.1 15M), we take the rough, unmarked path climbing above the *pista forestal*.

Strolls

(a) Capilerilla - Las Lomillas
From the village limit sign on the road down to **Pitres**, take the track on the left (Wp.11), then first left up another dirt track. Take the path on the right at the first left-hand bend then bear right at a Y-junction and take the tiny path immediately behind a venerable chestnut tree with partially exposed roots. Follow the faint paths climbing across terraced fields to a terrace with a small platform at the far end with metal poles supporting a sun-shelter and (possibly) a white caravan at the near end. Bear right at a narrow, recently dug irrigation channel and cut across the embankment to join the main walk down (a little below Wp.9).

(b) also see **Pista Forestal 4**.

We cross the driveway to the house and, when the path rejoins the *pista forestal* a couple of minutes later, bear left on a rough track through the forest.

When this track in turn rejoins the *pista forestal*, we follow the *pista forestal* for fifty metres and take another rough track through the forest on the left. After crossing the *pista forestal* for the third and last time, we take another rough track through the woods, which soon joins a waymarked path (Wp.2 29M), which we follow all the way to the *Área Recreativa*.

After passing an almost sheer outcrop of rock (Wp.3 35M), the path gets stonier and steeper. We bear left when the path joins a rough dirt track, which climbs to the *Área Recreativa* (Wp.4 45M).

Apart from what nature furnished, the *Área Recreativa* doesn't have a lot to recommend it since most of the infrastructure is unused, except for a green rubbish bin that's generally surrounded by a small mountain of refuse, some of it apparently animate. But don't let this put you off. Nature compensates admirably. The views are good and, to the left of the rubbish bin, a path winds down to a spectacular waterfall at the source of the **Río Bermejo**. On a hot day a shower is irresistible.

After refreshing ourselves here, we return to the *Área Recreativa* and continue on the dirt track up to **Pista Forestal 4**, where we turn left and, ignoring a dirt track doubling back on the right, follow **PF4** to the bridge over the **Junta de los Ríos** (Wp.5 55M, not shown on the map due to the proximity of Wp.4).

Woods below Junta de los Ríos

Extension

Turn right just after the bridge. Ten metres after a waypost with a black arrow on it, turn left on a rough 'way' (I hesitate to call it a path) marked with a blue paint arrow. Follow the ancient, thickly painted waymarks over the rocks to a natural 'jacuzzi' (Wp.6 10M from the bridge) between two waterfalls. Follow the waymarks, climbing past successive waterfalls to their source at the end of the **Acequia Baja** from the **Río Mulhacén**. Bear left under a large pine tree to the point where the *acequia* emerges from a large underground pipe, above which there's a track marked with black-arrowed wayposts. Go down the track one hundred metres (SSW), then turn left at another waypost onto a shaley path descending above a firebreak (E). The path bears SW for a while before swinging back (NE) towards the **Barranco del Jabalí** and descending to the waypost beside the bridge (Wp.5).

To return to Pórtugos (from Wp.5 55M)

Passing above a natural mirador thirty metres from the bridge, we follow **Pista Forestal 4** (W) for four hundred metres until two small cairns mark the narrow path (Wp.7 65M) down to **Capilerilla**, waymarked yellow five metres lower down. The path winds down through the forest passing occasional waymarks and the odd patch of water-erosion until it follows a stretch of concrete piping (Wp.8 75M) onto an exposed spit, just below which there's a waymarking post.

The waymarked path descends steadily, edging back towards the *río* before widening into a rough forestry track that joins another, better stabilised track above the **Acequia Ventajas Real** (Wp.9 95M) where there maybe a signpost indicating 'Bubíon 1h30/Pitres 1h' though this was uprooted and propped against a tree last time we passed. There's definitely a nice picnic spot though and another 'natural jacuzzi', twenty metres above the weir (to your left) on the southern side of the *acequia*.

... **Gaudiesque window frames.**

To descend to Capilerilla
We cross the *acequia*, either by the ford or the weir.

Ignoring the track on the right, we take the broad path descending through chestnuts, soon passing an eccentrically restored stone house, gaily painted and with Gaudiesque window frames.

The path narrows and bears left along another *acequia*, soon coming into view of the large house on the other side of the **Río Bermejo** (Wp.1), before crossing the *acequia* four times and emerging on a dirt track above a new house (Wp.10 104M).

This track rapidly descends to the eastern limit of **Capilerilla** (Wp.11 108M) where, due to private property and the configuration of the **Río Bermejo**, the official route chooses to follow the road to **Pórtugos** 1½ kilometres away. It's not possible to avoid all the road, but we can skip about two thirds of it.

Fifty metres before Wp.11, just after a recently built byre and a small *cortijo* with two chestnut trees, one with its roots exposed by erosion, we turn left onto a signposted path that doubles back below the *cortijo* then follows an *acequia* to a junction at a stone wall (Wp.12 120M).

Turning right with the *acequia* (possibly in it!) then left after fifteen metres, we descend, at first gradually then somewhat precipitously, to the road just before the bridge over the **Bermejo** (Wp.13 129M).

To avoid the dangerous bend just after the bridge, we take the slip path on the left, climb up to the **Secadero de Jamones Casa Juan**, then take the drive back down to the road. To finish the walk, we follow the road past the turning to **Atalbéitar** and turn left at the **Pórtugos** petrol station (Wp.14 140M) onto a concrete, lamplit track up to **Calle Rosario**.

The **Tahá de Pitres** was the local centre of the medieval silk trade, and still bears the marks in the abundance of mulberry trees off which the silk worms fed, and in the very name **Tahá**, an Arabic administrative district. It's famous for idyllic paths (in a region already famous for idyllic paths), exceptionally pretty villages (ditto), and stunning landscapes (ditto). After the touristy villages of the **Poqueira**, the **Tahá** is a welcome relief. Admittedly, it suffered like everywhere else from the sixties and seventies exodus to the industrial cities of the north and there are plenty of expats buying houses here, but the general atmosphere is still distinctively Alpujarran.

This particular walk threads its way through the higher villages of the **Tahá**, climaxing with the finest *mirador* in the valley, **La Mezquita**. The route follows the **GR7** from **Pitres** to **Busquístar** and the **GR-142** from **Busquístar** to below the **Mezquita**, completing the circuit with local trails. Most of it is waymarked and the walking is easy apart from the scramble up to the **Mezquita**. Park along the main road (gr-421) through the lower part of **Pitres**.

If you want to avoid slogging back up the road from **Atalbéitar** to **Pitres**, start from **Atalbéitar**. You could also easily start from any of the other villages. If you just want to visit the **Mezquita**, start from **Atalbéitar** and turn right at Wp.4.

N.B. The cartography identifies the highest point of the ridge between Wps.11 & 12 as the **Mezquita**. For the sake of ease and in accordance with local custom, I use 'the **Mezquita**' to refer to the ruins (Wp.11) at the tip of this ridge.

* 2 if you take the Walk 25 option at Wp.10, 3 if you climb the **Mezquita**.

** My timings seem much quicker than the official timings with the bizarre exception of the **Pórtugos - Busquístar** stretch where I took considerably longer! The official timings may have been done by different people, or just guessed at. In any case, the domesticity of the landscape means timings are less important for route-finding.

Strolls
(a) **Pitres - Fuente Agria** (Wps. 1-2)
(b) **Atalbéitar - the mill** (Wps. 3-4 + 13)
(c) **Pórtugos - Fuente Agria** (Wps. 6-7)
(d) The **Mezquita** from the road (gr-421). Take the dirt track 300 metres after the **GR7** leaves the road/800 metres from **Pórtugos Fuente Agria** (If coming from the east, 500 metres from the '*no potable*' *fuente* at the western limit of **Busquístar**). Bear left at the Y-junction, take the first path on the right then follow the ridge to the **Mezquita** (Wp.11). Return via the main walk to the dirt track (Wp.12), turn right for the road.

From the main road through **Pitres**, fifty metres above the **Hotel/Restaurant San Roque** and opposite a sign for 'Youth Hostel', we take the concrete alley descending next to a **GR7** waypost (Wp.1 0M).

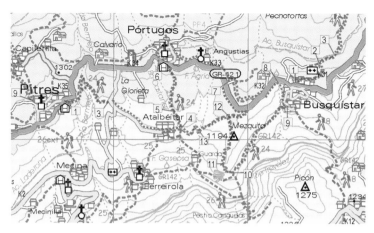

The concrete alley soon narrows to a dirt path passing under a tiny aqueduct beside the youth hostel/refuge, immediately after which two branches (Wp.2 5M) descend to cross the **Río Bermejo**. The official **GR7** route bears right and descends to a bridge. But for a less steep descent, we bear left, cross the little bridge over the *acequia* and, after a slightly larger bridge over a watercourse, take the path on the right down to the **Fuente Agria de Pitres** (an attractive plunge pool and tiny *fuente*), beyond which a narrow path past a ruined mill rejoins the **GR7**.

The **GR7** then climbs towards electricity pylons where it broadens to a dirt track joining the road to **Atalbéitar** (Wp.3 15M). Ten minutes on the road leads us down to the outskirts of **Atalbéitar**, where we pass the GR7 sign (Pitres 40') and Wp.1 of Walk 24. We cross the village via the **Calle Real**, the **Plaza Candelaria** and the **Calle El Horno** to emerge above the *lavadero* at the end of Walk 25, where we continue on the broad path heading east, signposted 'Pórtugos 30''.

After passing two stone huts, we climb to the bridge over the **Barranco del Castañar** and a junction of paths (Wp.4 29M). The path on the right is the return route and an option for a shorter walk from **Atalbéitar** to **La Mezquita**. For **Pórtugos**, we turn left and climb alongside the *barranco* on an old mule trail till it joins a new dirt track (Wp.5 35M).

We bear left here, then right fifty metres later, where a junction dips into the *barranco*. From here you can see the large white block of the **Hotel Nuevo Malagueño** in **Pórtugos**. When the track swings right, we continue past a large chestnut tree to pick up the old mule trail again. After a steepish climb along the mule trail, ignoring all the branches into fields, we bear left just below the road. The path crosses an evil looking effluent pipe, passes below the hotel garden and, judging by the bottle caps cobbling the path, the bar, too, before bearing right to join the main road (Wp.6 48M) at a **GR7** signpost ('Atalbéitar 30'').

We then cross the road and follow the concrete alley climbing into **Pórtugos**, taking the third turning on the right (at house Nº 9) into the **Plaza de la Iglesia**. We continue on the main street through the **Plaza Nueva**, passing the **Hostal/Bar Mirador**. After bearing right out of the **Plaza Nueva**, we leave the main street, turning left in front of the Telefonica installations onto the concrete track signposted 'Busquístar 15'. The track soon turns to dirt before descending to the road, which we'll follow for the next 500 metres. If you haven't yet tasted the ferruginous waters of the **Tahá**, it's worth pausing at the **Fuente Agria** next to the *ermita*, just after we join the road.

After the *fuente*, the road goes through a long bend to the right before joining a straight avenue of plane trees, at the end of which (Wp.7 68M), we take the broad path climbing to the left just before the road itself bends sharp left. (If you don't want to climb the **Mezquita**, 300 metres along the road a dirt track leads to Wp.12 and the **Mezquita** stroll).

Busquístar

After fifty metres the path bears right across an *acequia*. It then passes above fields of raspberries and cultivated blackberries, and goes through an overgrown section, before joining a dirt track behind a breeze-block byre, from where we can see **Busquístar**. The track descends alongside the road, crosses a stand of poplars, then joins the road which the **GR7** follows all the way into **Busquístar**.

We also follow the road, but ten metres before the village limits sign and (on our left) a *no potable fuente*, we leave the GR and turn right onto a dirt path descending steeply behind a black lamppost (Wp.8 89M).

The path descends into the lower part of **Busquístar** between another *no potable fuente* and a couple of concrete benches below shady plane trees. Beyond the *fuente*, we continue in the same direction down a concrete lane passing a sign for the 'Camino al Río & Ferreirola'. Descending at each junction, we pass **Las Lillas Bar**, after which a final steep descent emerges between a PR waypost and (hidden round the corner) a sign for the 'Camino a Ferreirola' (Wp.9 101M). We take the dirt path on the right towards **Ferreirola**. The path descends past a goat farm (your nose will tell you!) then climbs to briefly follow an *acequia*. Just after it crosses the *acequia*, peer through the trees ahead and you should be able to pick out some stone walls nestling in a rocky outcrop: this is the **Mezquita**.

After a level section alongside another *acequia*, the path joins a new dirt track down from the road. We climb the dirt track for fifty metres then, when it bears sharp right, take the old mule trail on the left, from where we can see the path beyond the *río* climbing the **Pechos de Carriguelas** (see Walk 26). Five minutes later, the path passes an overhanging rock and a concrete triangulation post, thirty metres after which there's a junction. Ignore the path descending on the left and take the path on the right towards **Ferreirola**.

If you don't want to climb the Mezquita
Follow this path to **Cortijo la Guarda** and return to **Atalbéitar** via Walk 25.

To climb the Mezquita
Take the Ferreirola path and, ten paces after the junction, next to an old red

arrow on a rock, turn right to follow a very faint path climbing between two small holm oaks (Wp.10 115M).

The path, marked by occasional red dots, is reasonably clear at first as it winds up past mini-terraces, but higher up it tends to get lost in brambles. After 4-5 minutes, about halfway up, you should find yourself faced with a red cross telling you not to climb straight ahead. In fact, though the path does bear right, it's so embrambled that you're better off ignoring the cross and going straight up to the right of the rocks for an easy scramble onto a clearer stretch of the path. Behind the cross, we bear left to traverse a slab of rock with a red line in the middle, and head towards a half-dead olive tree, shortly after which we reach the **Mezquita** (Wp.11 126M).

This is an exceptional site, well worth the climb, with the best views to be found anywhere in the valley. More recently, it's been used as a byre, but in Moorish times (possibly as far back as the eighth century) it was a stronghold controlling the passes over the **Sierra Mecina** that were vital to the silk trade: to the south is the **Carriguelas** pass (Walk 26), to the west the path snakes up from **Fondales** bridge (Walk 26), and to the east the **Busquístar** 'Camino al Río' (Walks 8 & 27). There's also a remarkable threshing circle built into a huge slab of rock.

To return to **Atalbéitar**, we will circle the valley dividing it from the **Mezquita**, passing the ruined mill perched on a promontory midway between the two. To start, we take the path between the buildings and the threshing circle, then cross the rock immediately below the **Mezquita** (N).

La Mezquita

Ducking under the skeleton of the chestnut tree directly behind the **Mezquita**, we then follow the waymarks along the ridge, climbing onto the rocks just to the left of another concrete triangulation post, and squeezing between the boulders at the highest point of the ridge (the cartographic **Mezquita**).

After the 'peak', litter and beer cans mark the favoured picnic spot of the agricultural labourers who work the nearby fields. The path crosses the fields within sight of the road and the avenue of trees (Wp.7) to join a dirt track (Wp.12 141M) where we turn left and, when the track bears left some fifty metres later, continue straight ahead onto a path between the fields. Two fields later, the path dips to the left of a small house with a pretty garden. We bear right below the garden onto a narrower, shadier stretch.

After descending past another little house, we bear right again at a junction beside a waypost (Wp.13 150M) shortly before the mill. Five minutes after winding round the mill promontory, we come to the junction with the **GR7** (Wp.4). We return to **Atalbéitar** and/or **Pitres** on the **GR7**.

A ferruginous spring

Four linked strolls between the lower villages of the **Tahá** along pleasant, peaceful, easy paths and mule trails with one slightly rougher section between **Fondales** and **Ferreirola**. Ferreirola is the last toponymal link with another phenomenon for which **La Tahá** is famed, the extraordinarily high iron content of its springs, which give the water such a distinctive taste (hence the **Fuentes Agrias** at **Pitres** and **Portúgos**; *agrio* meaning sour) and lends the riverbeds their startling ochre tint - some rocks literally seem to be bleeding rust. The **Tahá**'s original name was *Ferreira*.

This route is ideal for a relaxing day after some of the more strenuous mountain walks. In summer, keep an eye open for the pungent white-flowered oregano. All these traditional routes between villages are peppered with slip paths into the fields. Unless otherwise stated, always stick to the main path. For simplicity's sake, I use 'path' to describe all the routes taken, though several would qualify as mule trails. Park along the road leading into **Atalbéitar**.

* if anything's open, which it probably won't be, in which case 0. The **Al Jipe** bar in **Mecinilla** and the hotel in **Mecina** are more reliable and are only about 10 minutes away from **Fondales**.

N.B. Since many people will probably want to break this up into shorter strolls, waypoint timings are given between villages, not on the basis of the entire walk. You'll probably take longer than the stated time, not because you have to stop to catch your breath or because we went belting round like maniacs, but because you'll want to savour the tranquillity of the place.

Strolls
(a) **Ferreirola - Fuente Gaseosa/Cortijo la Guarda** (Wps. 8-9) **GR142**
(b) **Ferreirola - Río Bermejo** (Wps. 3-4) **GR142**
(c) **Fondales - Río Bermejo** (Wp.4) **GR142**
(d) **Fondales - Roman Bridge** (Wp.6) **GR142**

Atalbéitar - Ferreirola 15 minutes
Ferreirola - Fondales 20 - 25 minutes
Fondales - Ferreirola 30 - 40 minutes
Ferreirola - Atalbéitar 35 minutes

ATALBÉITAR - FERREIROLA

From the first house on the western edge of **Atalbéitar** (Wp.1 0M), we take the short concrete drive down towards the dark red doors and immediately

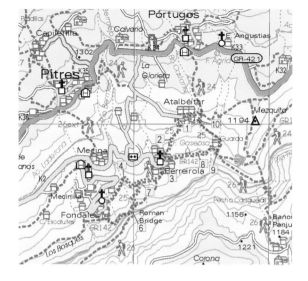

bear right onto a dirt path winding down past almond groves, agave, blackberry and mulberry. After crossing an *acequia* (Wp.2 7M), we bear left below a peach and plum orchard within sight of **Ferreirola** church. We then pass a long, narrow waterhut and the path broadens, bringing us into **Ferreirola** a little over ten minutes from **Atalbéitar**.

Maintaining direction into **Ferreirola**, we pass between a *lavadero* and the **Villa Kiko**, then follow the alley descending below the church square, passing on our left the **Calle El Cerezo**, the **Villa Paquita** and **Los Monteros** before climbing slightly to reach a tiny stone cabin beside a signpost, 'GR142 Mecina-Fondales 30 mins' (Wp.3 21M).

Before proceeding, it's worth peering over the cabin door to see a magnificent old clay oven.

The sign at Wp.3

FERREIROLA - FONDALES

Fifteen metres after the GR sign, the path bears left at a waypost, and winds down above an olive grove. At a Y-junction halfway along the olive grove, we take the upper path climbing past a fig tree, shortly after which we see **Fondales** ahead.

After descending over a rocky section, the path winds along the slopes through tangled blackberry bushes and dense *retama* dotted with occasional acacia, olive, chestnut and fig trees. Climbing slightly between huge rocks it crosses a concrete bridge (Wp.4 9M) over the **Río Bermejo**.

A brief climb past some poplars precedes a section between an *acequia* and another olive grove before we cross the *acequia* and continue past an immense chestnut tree and a water reservoir. The path follows another *acequia* till, about fifty metres after the chestnut tree, we dip down below the *acequia* (Wp.5 15M) and descend to a stream and a tiny *fuente* with benches, a few minutes from **Fondales**.

In **Fondales**, we bear left after the **GR142** waypost ('Ferreirola 30 mins') to descend along the outskirts of the village. We keep bearing left till we pass underneath a broad *tinao* with brown garage doors on the left, immediately after which we see a GR142 sign 'Órgiva 5h30 mins'.

FONDALES - FERREIROLA

We follow the **GR142** concreted lane down past a *fuente/lavadero* where it turns into a dirt path. The subsequent descent is clear except for one slightly ambiguous moment where the path divides next to a pomegranate tree with a prickly pear bush behind it. We take the narrower, rougher path to the left, descending through a small poplar wood to an idyllic spot beside a Roman bridge (Wp.6 10M) over the **Río Trevélez**.

Bearing left at the bridge, we leave the **GR142** and follow the right bank of the **Río Trevélez**, almost immediately crossing a stream over large slabs of smooth stone. Beyond the stream, a yellow waymark indicates a rough path that zigzags up through big bushes of *retama*.

Plunge pool above Wp.6

We follow this path, crossing an eroded, rocky section and climbing towards a small chestnut tree where there's a very old, very faint yellow dot on a rock, and the path becomes clearer. After winding through a small stand of chestnut, the path climbs steeply then bears right on a gentler slope below a long rocky outcrop topped with a couple of dead chestnuts.

The rocks give way to stone retaining walls until the path bears left then right to pass a partially dead chestnut, after which it winds up below an acacia to rejoin the outward route (Wp.7 24M). Turning right here, we reach **Ferreirola** five minutes later, where we retrace our steps to the church square.

If you started this route from **Fondales** or the Roman bridge, you'll find the church by continuing straight on past the GR sign and bearing left after the **Villa Paquita** to climb to the *fuente/lavadero* next to the church square.

From the *fuente/lavadero*, we follow the GR waymarks in the lane below the **Villa Kiko (Calle Rosario)** across **Ferreirola** until **Calle Rosario** bears right and then left to join the path marked 'Busquístar 50 mins'.

FERREIROLA- ATALBÉITAR

A few minutes from **Ferreirola**, we come to the celebrated **Fuente La Gaseosa** (Wp.8 3M), decorated with ceramics depicting the seasons. At least a sip of its extraordinary tasting waters is obligatory.

After the *fuente*, we cross the bridge over the **Barranco del Castañar** and follow a broad path above a large threshing circle before climbing to cross another bridge over the watercourse from **Pórtugos' Fuente Agria**.

Fifty metres later, a third bridge leads onto an open sheet of rock, **Cortijo de la Guarda** (Wp.9 15M), with fine views down the **Río Trevélez**. The **GR142** continues east, linking up with Walk 24.

Fuente La Gaseosa

Immediately after **Cortijo La Guarda**, we leave the GR and take the clear path on the left (NE) up to another junction, where we bear left again. Climbing steeply, we cross the **Fuente Agria** watercourse again, after which the gradient moderates and we come into a shady area.

After crossing an *acequia*, we follow the main path up past various branches until it emerges from the tree cover, where it swings left and climbs alongside a terracing wall to another bridge over the **Barranco del Castañar** (Wp.10 30M).

We cross the *barranco* and an *acequia* to climb a narrow, possibly water-logged path densely lined with brambles. Just after a sign on the left saying 'Propiedad Particular - Ganado', we bear right, away from a terrace (Wp.11 32M) and climb to **Atalbéitar** fifty metres later. Turn left to cross the village and return to Wp.1 (35M).

An easy walk (despite the extraordinary descent after Wp.5) using the GR142, dirt tracks and PRs, and taking in two of the Moorish silk-route passes. The views are spectacular. *Cabra montés* can occasionally be seen near **La Corona** (see map). And it's worth pausing at Wp.6; the bridge appears to be man-made, but in fact is built on a natural arc of rock spanning the spectacular gorge. Park in the tiny car-park at the entrance to **Fondales** or if full, a little way up the road.

| 3 | 3H * | 9 km | ↗ 400m ↘ 400m | ↻ | 🍴 3 ** |

* add 30 minutes either way if descending from **Pitres**.
** as per Walk 25

Access by bus: If arriving by bus, the track from **Pitres** to **Fondales** starts on the main road opposite the **Paseo Maritimo**. Take the concrete lane to the right of **La Meta** restaurant and follow the mule trail down to **Mecina** (15M). Bear left on the concrete lane into **Mecina**, then take either the second or third turning on the right down to the *Ayuntamiento de la Tahá* noticeboard. Bear right, and follow the road round the hotel and church down to **Mecinilla** (20M). Enter **Mecinilla** to the right of **Al Jipe** bar and follow the main alley to a *fuente* dated '1964'. Bear left, then right, then left again to join the path to **Fondales**. At the road take the path on the right of the garage with red and white doors down to **Fondales** car-park (Wp.1 30M; subsequent times from 0M).

> **Stroll**
> **Fondales - Mecinilla**
> Climb along the road, return via the path.
>
> **Access by car:** 1km west of the junction of the **Trevélez/Torviscón** roads (see Walk 8 Wp.11) take the dirt track along the **Sierra Mecina** and/or down to the **Baños de Panjuila**. The main track can be used by cars from Wp.4 to Wp.3 and beyond.

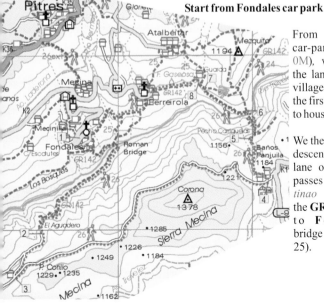

Start from Fondales car park

From **Fondales** car-park (Wp.1 0M), we follow the lane into the village and take the first right next to house Nº3.

We then continue descending till a lane on the left passes under a *tinao* and joins the **GR142** down to **Fondales** bridge (see Walk 25).

Fondales Bridge

Crossing the bridge, we follow the **GR142** (SW) as it climbs above the river on a broad, easy path. Twenty minutes from the bridge, the path crosses a rockslide then zigzags up **El Aguadero** to join the end of a rough dirt track (Wp.2 45M).

We follow the dirt track up behind a newly built house to join the main **Sierra Mecina** dirt track (Wp.3 55M). Leaving the **GR142**, which bears right for a long, dry, dreary drag down to **Órgiva** (it's all tarmac and *retama* - if you want to go to **Órgiva**, get a bus), we turn left to follow the track along the **Sierra Mecina**.

The track climbs gently with fine views of the **Tahá**, the cliffs of **Carriguelas** and **Helechones**, and the old iron mines at **Cerro Conjuro**, before descending toward a group of houses just above the **Trevélez-Torviscón** road (L-9).

At the houses, just before Number 4, we take the wayposted track on the left (Wp.4 95M) to descend past the ruins of the *Baños de Panjuila* (on our right and virtually imperceptible) to the cliffs of the **Pecho de las Carriguelas** or **Carihuelas** (Wp.5 105M) where the track turns into a path.

The houses before waypoint 4

If you want to picnic, there's an ideal spot on the left just before the descent, among ash and poplar in a couple of tiny cliff top fields. There are also pleasant terraces at the bottom, on the left just before the bridge.

From the top, it's hard to believe there's a way down to the river, but in fact an easy path zigzags down causing no difficulty, even for those who suffer acute vertigo. We cross the bridge (Wp.6 125M) and take the path climbing past the ruined mill.

Ignoring a branch on the right ten metres later (climbing to **La Mezquita** and **Busquístar** - see Walk 24), we stay on the main path to pass another waypost and a ruined cabin before rejoining the **GR142** (Wp.7 135M).

Bearing left here, we cross the rock shelf at the **Cortijo de la Guarda** (Wp.8 136M) and follow the **GR142** (Walk 25 in the opposite sense) across a series of watercourses to the **Fuente Agria** and **Ferreirola**. After the first *tinao*, turn right up an alley that immediately bears left and crosses **Ferreirola** to the *fuente/lavadero* in front of the church. To return to **Fondales,** follow Walk 25 back.

A glorious, wild walk exploring a little-known, scarcely visited end of the **Tahá**, climbing to the **Cerillos Negros** firewatch hut to take in stunning views of the **Trevélez Gorge**, then descending by the easternmost 'silk-route' pass over the **Sierra Mecina**. The only drawback is that it also involves a couple of kilometres on the road. There's very little traffic though, the views from the road are excellent, and the ascent and descent out of and into the **Tahá** are so exceptional, I suspect most walkers would happily do double the distance on the road. *Helecho* means bracken or fern, not that it's much in evidence nowadays. Park in the main square in **Busquístar**.

4   3H   8 km   550m / 550m   4*

* in **Busquístar**

Buses back: if you don't want to do the full circuit, the bus passes Wp.7 at about 5.20pm.

From the main square in **Busquístar**, we take the concrete lane to the right of the **Bar Vargas** then the first dirt track on the left, signposted

Short version
- to the bridge (Wp.5) 50 minutes (one-way)

Strolls
(a) follow the start to the threshing circle for fine views up the valley
(b) **Los Cerillos Negros**. Just over 7km from **Trevélez** bridge (dir. **Juviles**) turn right on the **Cástaras/Torviscón** road (Wp.7) and park 1km later at (Wp.10). Follow the road BACK to Wp.8 then follow the described walk to return to the car.

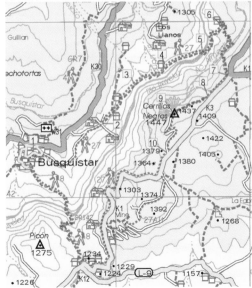

'Camino Helechal' (Wp.1 0M). Sticking to the main track, we ignore all branches as it climbs gently to a threshing circle from where we can see the **Cerillos Negros** firewatch hut.

We then follow the increasingly narrow dirt track as it passes behind a two-storey concrete house and ignore all branches until we come to a cross-roads (Wp.2 13M) with a new dirt track. The track we've been following continues on the far side as a narrow path that eventually leads to **Los Llanos**.

We, however, bear right on the new dirt track to pass behind a white-painted *cortijo*, beyond which a narrow path descends to a second, gated *cortijo*. Immediately after the gate, there are two paths on the right. We take the second path to pass below the pasture in front of the *cortijo* and descend (NE) towards the river.

Fifty metres above the river, we bear right at a Y-junction (Wp.3 31M) and descend to another gate, after which the path dips and rises across the watercourses of the **Barrancos del Tesoro** and **de los Llanos** before climbing steeply to a third gate. We continue climbing to a small chestnut tree then bear right, heading upriver to pass in front of a ruin (Wp.4 40M).

From the ruin, we descend to a small wood where the path is eroded by a couple of torrents. Beyond the wood, there's yet another gate, after which a gentle climb and brief descent lead to the bridge (Wp.5 49M), which looks terrifying as you approach but seems solid enough once you're on it. Beyond the bridge, a clear path climbs below the cliffs to cross a meagre watercourse next to a ruin (Wp.6 61M) (visible from before the bridge) where the way up to **Portichuelo** begins.

It's worth pausing here, partly for a breather beneath the ruin's shady walnut tree, partly to enjoy the fine views back towards **Busquístar**, but also to orient yourself. If you look up from directly behind the ruin, you can see some of the concrete crash barrier along the **Trevélez** road and, to the south, the firewatch hut. Like most climbs, this one's a lot easier than it looks.

We take the path that bears right behind the ruin to re-cross the watercourse a little higher up, after which it climbs steeply, hopefully passing occasional cairns. If the cairns have been knocked down, stick to the clearer traces (most of the others are shortcuts) as they wind up to cross the broad **Acequia de Almegíjar** in a little under fifteen minutes.

Beyond the *acequia*, the increasingly broad and clear path continues climbing, meandering through some massive rocks before emerging at the junction of the **Trevélez-Juviles** & **Torviscón** roads (Wp.7 85M).

Turning right, we follow the **Torviscón** road for just under 300 metres. As it comes into a slight rise, we leave the road to take a faint path on the right (Wp.8 91M) climbing through the pine trees.

The path soon loses definition, but if you stick to the right of the pine wood, a series of goat tracks along the ridge lead up to a little pass between two rocky outcrops where the path becomes clearer, winding along the cliff tops (near enough for gawping, far enough for comfort) before climbing gently to the firewatch tower (Wp.9 102M) for exceptional views of the **Trevélez Gorge** from its headwaters all the way down to the western end of the **Tahá de Pitres**.

To descend from the firewatch hut, we take the dirt track down to the road (Wp.10 110M), where we have a choice of routes to the mule trail/**GR142** back to **Busquístar**. It's quicker, easier and quite as attractive to follow the road (2.3km). However, if you're a purist and will not walk on tarmac without some overwhelming compulsion, you can take the alternative route across the old iron mines of **Cerro del Conjuro**. Be warned though: this is very rough walking, frequently off-path, and virtually indescribable! I'll do my best though.

Busquístar

The start is easy enough. We follow the road for a hundred metres then, as it winds into an S-bend, bear left onto the chained dirt track into the mines. After crossing the first extraction site, we bear right on a broad gravel track passing a solitary stand of holm oak.

At the remains of a small concrete hut from where we can see **Busquístar**, we bear left to follow a well-trodden goat track running alongside abandoned telegraph poles till it bears right and disappears amid the scrub next to a small rocky outcrop.

To the left of this outcrop, an infinitesimal goat trail descends to a clearly visible, denuded platform, from where we can see another S-bend in the road, which is our next objective. We now descend through another area of scrub at the edge of this platform to a dirt track ten metres below, from where a succession of dirt tracks appear to wind down nicely to the road - they don't.

The first four dirt-tracks/terraces don't link up, so instead we have to maintain a westerly direction for some VERY rough walking along a series of goat tracks so faint they're virtually invisible. After the fourth terrace-track, we can follow the dirt tracks, but not all the way to the road.

Just as the dirt track comes back into view of **Busquístar**, about one hundred metres above the road and the roofless ruins of the mine works, we abandon the track and take another VERY rough 'way' (it's not a path but there are occasional stretches churned up by the goats) zigzagging down toward the ruins, just to the right of which, some steps hidden by clumps of *retama*, lead down to the lowermost track and the road.

We then follow the road for the last few hundred metres to the **GR142** at the junction with the L-9 to **Cástaras**, about half-an-hour from Wp.10. From here it takes 30-40 minutes to return to **Busquístar**: see Walk 8 Wps. 11-13.

Yes, if you know any Spanish, it does mean what you think it means. If you don't, *culo perro* is an indelicate way of describing a dog's bottom. I don't care to delve into the toponymy of this, but despite the name it's a fine walk made exceptional if you have the pathfinding skills to link it with the lower half of Walk 29. It's especially worthwhile finding the way down in summer as returning via the shady river path is cooler than staying on the exposed path above the **Crestones de los Posteros**. If you do take the 'link' please add to the cairns. Apart from the walk through the village, the way up is nearly all gentle climbing. Due to their proximity, Wps. 9&10 are marked by a single waypoint symbol on the map. If you intend doing the loop, park in the **Plaza de la Iglesia**. If not, park in the **Plaza Barrío Medio** and follow Walk 30 through the village. To reach the parking spots from the main square/tourist strip, take the road signposted for the *ayuntamiento* up past the Spar supermarket, until it bears round towards **Restaurante Casa Julio**. Carry straight on for the **Plaza de la Iglesia**. For the **Barrio Medio**, turn left after the restaurant and then sharp right when you come to the hostal and **Jamones Fernando**.

2* | 3H 10M | 9 km | 400m / 400m | 5 (↻)

* once out of the village!   **in **Trevélez**

Stroll
Bear left at Wp.2 for a pleasant stroll up through pasture meadows.

From the **Plaza de la Iglesia** in **Trevélez' Barrío Bajo**, we take the aptly named **Calle Cuesta** ('Hill Street') up to a T-junction next to a *fuente* with a bench carved in the rock. We turn left here, then right fifty metres later, to climb a cobbled lane up to **Calle Carcel**.

The path at waypoint 1

We then take the narrow concrete alley to the left of the *comidas/camas/jamones* sign, turn right on **Calle Horno**, left at the *lavadero*, then take the first path on the left (Wp.1 0M). The path - in fact broad enough to qualify as a mule trail - climbs steadily to a Y-junction (Wp.2 10M) beside a stand of poplars, where we bear right to

continue on the main trail, climbing past two *cortijos* and ignoring occasional branches into fields.

Fifty metres after the mule trail passes between a large stone *cortijo* (on the left) and a byre (on the right), we ignore the waymarked route on the left up

The path north after Wp.3

to **Siete Lagunas** (Wp.3 42M) and continue along the mule trail (N), which soon dwindles to a dirt path. The path becomes stonier and drier, gradually climbing to pass a plaque (Wp.4 74M) commemorating two *Guardia Civiles* killed in 1957 in a gun battle with one of the guerrilla groups that took to the mountains after the civil war and stayed there for the next twenty-odd years.

It then winds up to cross the **Crestones de los Posteros** into the **Río Culo Perro** valley, where it gradually descends (NW) to a Y-junction (Wp.5 85M). We take the right-hand branch descending into the valley to a faint cow path branching off to the right (Wp.6 88M) marked by a large cairn, I hope - I certainly built one, anyway.

Fine views south en route

To return by the same route
If you intend returning by the same route, stay on the main path and descend to the **Río Culo Perro** (Wp.7 95M) next to a rough wooden bridge, beyond which the path climbs to the **Cortijo de las Vacas**.

To link up with the Río Trevélez
To link up with the **Río Trevélez**, we take the cow path at Wp.6. Beware though, you need good route finding skills. What follows is a lot of detail for a very short distance, but there's only one way down that doesn't involve blundering through brambles or pitching over five metre drops, so hopefully every word is justified. Look down to the junction of the **Ríos Culo Perro** and **Trevélez**. On the left bank of the **Río Culo Perro**, there's a large, intensely green meadow. On the right bank, an escarpment climbs away from the meadow, culminating fifty metres above the river in an outcrop of rock, just to the right of which, you should be able to pick out a threshing circle. This is our first objective

From the cairn, we follow the cow path along the flank of the valley (SE), crossing a shallow depression, after which the path descends slightly towards a grassy platform in front of the white-fronted **Cortijo Encinilla** on the other side of the river. The cow path then heads in a more easterly direction, dividing just above the grassy platform. We can't see the threshing circle from here, but stick to the higher traces of the path as it swings back to the right (SE), after which the threshing circle comes into view again.

Just before it bears round onto a rocky ridge, we abandon the cow path at a point marked by a second cairn (Wp.8 104M - all subsequent times exclude the time between Wps. 6&7) and zigzag down the scrubby/scree slope towards the threshing circle, taking care to keep above the taller scrub running up from the river. There's an old barbed-wire fence just above the threshing circle with a gate in the middle, beyond which a very faint path descends directly to the threshing circle, about five metres from the cow path.

Bearing round to the right of the threshing circle, we come to the remains of an old cabin built into the rock. We then descend between the ruined cabin wall and another outcrop of rock (NE) down to a solitary holm oak and a broken barbed-wire fence above the junction of the rivers.

Crossing the barbed-wire fence, we maintain a north-easterly direction toward the river junction and another large cairn (Wp.9 116M) thirty metres below the barbed-wire fence. We bear left here and follow a <u>very</u> faint trail (NW) until we see another cairn, still on the right bank of the **Río Culo Perro**, on a small grassy knoll below a large poplar. Don't be tempted by any previous 'shortcuts' down to the river - they all end up in brambles. The 'trail' bears right then zigzags down to the cairn (Wp.10 126M).

After fording the **Río Culo** Perro (you may have to take your boots off in Spring), we descend through the meadow seen from Wp.6, passing in front of a semi-abandoned *cortijo* and crossing a marshy dell to a ford over the **Río Trevélez** fifteen metres upriver.

After the ford, a rough gate in a barbed-wire fence (Wp.11 131M) leads onto a heavily water-logged path (you might be forgiven for thinking you were walking *in* the river rather than alongside it) and a ten minute descent to a bridge over the river, just next to the source of the **Acequia Nueva**.

We cross the *acequia* twice and, fifty metres after the second crossing, bear left, away from the *acequia* and back towards the river. We then stay on the right bank of the river all the way to **Trevélez**. It may sometimes be flooded, especially in spring, but don't be beguiled onto the left bank by apparently drier routes: they all end in deep fords with swift currents. (See Walk 29, Wps. 7-1 for details.) It takes about one hour to reach **Trevélez** from Wp.11.

A straightforward walk, following the **Río Trevélez** from the domestic landscape near the village up to the wilder area below **El Horcajo**, a traditional pasture where, according to Gerald Brenan, shepherds were once wont to set upon unwary travellers and relieve them of anything relievable.

The Río Trevélez valley

Fortunately, times have changed but the landscape remains the same. The only drawback is that, even though the river may be dry in summer between Wps. 3&6, much of the path is often flooded; not enough to impede progress, but sufficient to qualify as a river itself anywhere else.

The Río Trevélez

Take a towel; there are fine plunge-pools throughout, though beware of slippery rocks. Park in the **Plaza de la Iglesia** (see Walk 28).

2/3* 4½ H 14 km 600m 600m 5

* to **Hoya del Chordí** 2 : to the headwaters 3   ** in **Trevélez**

From the **Plaza de la Iglesia** in **Trevélez' Barrío Bajo**, we take the **Calle Cuesta** and turn right immediately behind the church (Wp.1 0M) onto the broad dirt track down to the river. One hundred metres after the track crosses a watercourse, we bear left onto a narrow dirt path (Wp.2 5M) that descends to the river twenty minutes later.

Bearing left at a Y-junction (Wp.3 28M), we climb briefly before rejoining the river above a series of small, improvised dams. After fording a shallow affluent (Wp.4 40M) and splashing along a section resembling an *acequia* (Wp.5 45M) (it _is_ still the path), we bear right on a bank of raised earth by-passing a meadow.

The path then climbs briefly to follow the **Acequia Nueva** before crossing a rough bridge (Wp.6 55M) shortly after which we have to cross the *acequia* again and take a larger bridge onto the river's left bank. For the second

Expect to get your feet wet!

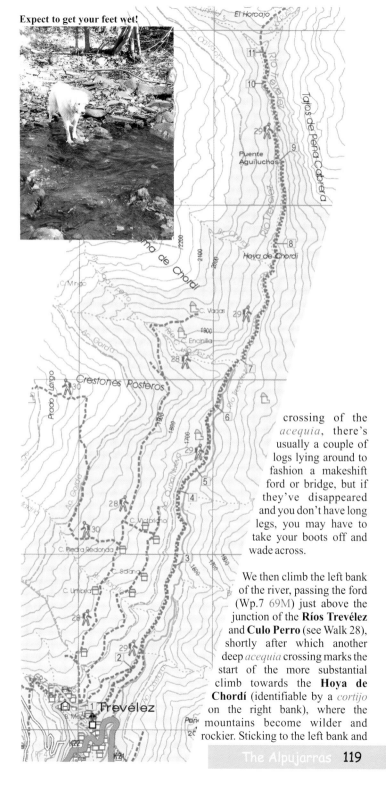

crossing of the *acequia*, there's usually a couple of logs lying around to fashion a makeshift ford or bridge, but if they've disappeared and you don't have long legs, you may have to take your boots off and wade across.

We then climb the left bank of the river, passing the ford (Wp.7 69M) just above the junction of the **Ríos Trevélez** and **Culo Perro** (see Walk 28), shortly after which another deep *acequia* crossing marks the start of the more substantial climb towards the **Hoya de Chordí** (identifiable by a *cortijo* on the right bank), where the mountains become wilder and rockier. Sticking to the left bank and ignoring all branches away from the river, we descend into the **Hoya de Chordí** along a water-logged path.

The Río Trevélez

The path loses definition in a meadow beneath a large shady ash with a cow's skull hanging halfway up its trunk (Wp.8 101M), but maintaining direction we soon pick up a badly eroded rock-laid stretch running alongside the river below the meadow.

After splashing through another flooded stretch, we cross another small *acequia* and descend on a drier stretch to the river below the **Tajos de Peña Cabrera**.

From here, if you look up towards the **Horcajo** at the end of the valley, you can see a small white building, which is about a hundred metres above our destination. The path continues along alternately dry and waterlogged sections till it crosses a very rudimentary wood and slate bridge (**Puente de los Aguiluchos**, Wp.9 127M) and, five minutes later, crosses back onto the left bank by a smaller slightly sturdier bridge.

After the second bridge, a succession of steady climbs leads up to the junction of the **Ríos Juntillas** and **Puerto de Jeres** that form the **Río Trevélez**. En route, there's a junction of paths marked with cairns (Wp.10 151M). We ignore the path on the right (the way to **Jeres de Marquesado**) and bear left on the main path to reach the junction of the rivers five minutes later (Wp.11 155M).

Our return by the same route takes two hours.

Bit of a marathon this one, but amply rewarded by a real sense of wilderness above **Campiñuela** and access to one the Alpujarras' most celebrated sites, the **Seven Lagoons**. Needless to say, the views are stunning throughout. So's the climbing! The upper reaches of the **Río Culo Perro** (Wp.5) are worth visiting even if you don't do the final climb to the lagoons. And if you're really feeling lazy, you can join one of the horse-riding excursions up to **Las Chorreras** and walk to the lagoons from there (contact 'Rutas a Caballo' in **Barrío Alto**, **Trevélez** 958 858 601). The path is clear, except briefly after Wp.4 & between Wps.7-9. The descent from the **Mirador de Trevélez**, is an attractive route that also links the **Poqueira** and **Trevélez** gorges, but don't do it in reverse. The ingredients of a stimulating if knee-breaking descent would be dreary misery as a climb. The clear path from Wp.7 is another classic ascent of the **Mulhacén** that takes around three hours.

* 5 – though not so long, this is every bit as tough as Walk 22 and climbs even further (1600m). If you think that sounds rough, you may like to bear in mind that every August there's a race (this is not a joke) from **Trevélez** to the **Mulhacén**, a 2000 metre climb; last year the quickest lunatics did it in under 3 hours!

** 7 hours 10 mins for the full circuit, but given the distance and climbing involved, allow 10 hours

Laguna Hondera: 7 hours 10 mins, but likewise, allow 8 hours

*** in **Trevélez**

> **Short Version**
> - to the headwaters of the **Río Culo Perro** (Wp.4/5) 6½ hours there and back.

The signpost after Wp.3

The start is the same as for Walk 28, but since we don't return via the **Río Trevélez**, we start from the **Plaza Barrío Medio**. Parking is limited in the square itself, but there's usually plenty of room further back on the road down towards the **Barrío Bajo**.

Taking the narrow street past the excellent **Panadería Federico**, we turn left at the 'comidas/camas/jamones' sign, right on **Calle Horno**, left at the *lavadero*, then take the first path on the left (Wp.1 0M). We then follow Walk 28 to Wp.3 (42M) and bear left at the 'Campiñuela/7 Lagunas' signpost to climb a clear path

Looking south, near the start of the walk

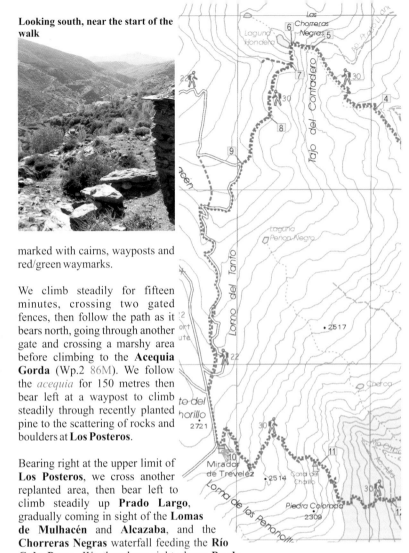

marked with cairns, wayposts and red/green waymarks.

We climb steadily for fifteen minutes, crossing two gated fences, then follow the path as it bears north, going through another gate and crossing a marshy area before climbing to the **Acequia Gorda** (Wp.2 86M). We follow the *acequia* for 150 metres then bear left at a waypost to climb steadily through recently planted pine to the scattering of rocks and boulders at **Los Posteros**.

Bearing right at the upper limit of **Los Posteros**, we cross another replanted area, then bear left to climb steadily up **Prado Largo**, gradually coming in sight of the **Lomas de Mulhacén** and **Alcazaba**, and the **Chorreras Negras** waterfall feeding the **Río Culo Perro**. We then bear right above **Prado Largo** for a gentler climb to the small cabin and large threshing circle at **Cortijo de la Campiñuela** (Wp.3 133M), frequently misplaced on maps.

The path continues past the ruined walls of the **Campiñuela** byre (NW), crossing a tiny rivulet above a small reservoir. It then climbs (at first steadily then more gently) to cross a narrow torrent, after which another steady climb leads to the **Río Culo Perro** just above a narrow dike (Wp.4 165M), sometimes called **El Vertedero**.

We can either follow the path till it crosses the river fifty metres later or (as mapped) cross the dyke and head upriver toward the **Tajo del Contadero** cliffs to pick up a fainter stony path climbing away from the river toward the **Chorreras**.

Now we follow the cairns up to a minor affluent of the **Culo Perro** (Wp.5 197M) where a climb that has so far been at the upper limit of 'steady' suddenly turns 'steep' - and nasty! But don't be discouraged; it's tough, but not as tough as it looks.

Crossing the affluent, we climb alongside the cascade, looking out for the cairns where the path disappears under rockfalls, and soon (certainly sooner than seems possible from Wp.5) come to **Laguna Hondera** (Wp.6 216M), the largest and, despite what some maps claim, lowest of the seven lagoons tucked into the glaciation cirque defined by the **Lomas de Mulhacén** and **Alcazaba**.

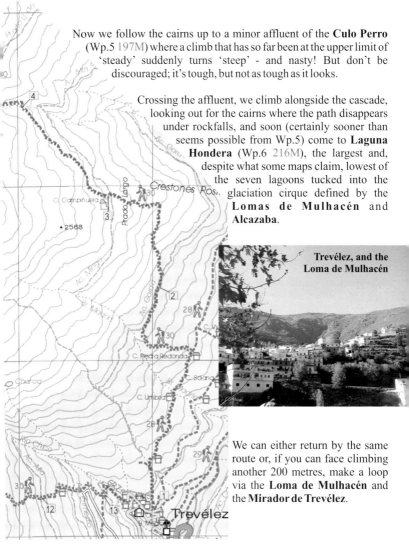

Trevélez, and the Loma de Mulhacén

We can either return by the same route or, if you can face climbing another 200 metres, make a loop via the **Loma de Mulhacén** and the **Mirador de Trevélez**.

Loma de Mulhacén and Mirador de Trevélez loop

On the south-east tip of the ridge round the cirque, there's a tall thin cairn. At first glance there's no way up to this, but in fact to the south-east of the **Laguna Hondera**, behind a large rock and a small windbreak (commonly known, a tad rosily to my mind, as the **Refugio Natural de Siete Lagunas**), a very faint 'way' that gradually becomes something approximating a path, does wind up past the tall thin cairn to another fatter cairn built on a large rock (Wp.7 227M).

Ignoring the clear path climbing to the right along the **Cuesta** or **Cuerda de Resuello**, we head south-west from the fat cairn to cross the first of two shallow depressions or *hoyas* that lead to the **Llanos del Mulhacén**. There's neither path nor cairns to begin with, so you'll have to take my word for this, but after a couple of hundred metres you'll come to the first of a series of cairns marking the way and a slightly clearer path. You'll also probably see plenty of *cabras montés*.

Bear right as you cross this first *hoya*, staying near its upper/western limit to traverse the higher patches of grass just below the shallow cliffs, where you should find the first cairns. Maintaining a south-westerly direction, we cross a broad grassy stretch on the far side of the *hoya* to pass two cairns marking a reasonably clear trail which climbs slightly before bearing left up to a large cone-shaped cairn. The path virtually disappears again here, but faint traces and a series of tall cairns indicate the way out of the first *hoya* onto a ridge overlooking the second shallower and stonier *hoya* (Wp.8 243M).

The stones are smaller here, so the trodden way is slightly clearer, and is also well marked with cairns. Again we circle round the head of the *hoya*, climbing gently to its highest recess, where a steeper path, just discernible from Wp.8, climbs out of the *hoya* in a SSE direction onto a scree slope where it disappears. We bear right here and follow the cairns off-path (W) as the slope gradually levels out and leads up to the **Mulhacén** branch of the **Carretera de Veleta** (Wp.9 260M). We then follow this track (see Walk 22 for a generic description) to the **Mirador de Trevélez** (Walk 22 Wp.17).

Bearing left at a waypost marking the *mirador*, we leave the *carretera* to cross bare ground to another waypost at the top of the path (Wp.10 320M) down to **Trevélez** (visible below). We then follow this path, ignoring both the tracks over the rocky ridge to the south (the **Loma de los Penoncillos**) AND, if you care for your knees, the various shortcuts (a 1300 metre descent in 3km really doesn't need shortcuts, as well).

The path is well wayposted, passing the abandoned *cortijo* and threshing circle of the **Corral del Chorillo** (Wp.11 370M), and crossing first an *acequia* (Wp.12 400M) then, a hundred metres below, a dirt track. It then descends to a ruin (currently being rebuilt), below which it crosses private land, passing three gates before emerging on another dirt track at a bend above two threshing circles. We take the wayposted path between the threshing circles for a final descent to the **GR7** (Wp.13 425M) five minutes from **Barrío Alto** in **Trevélez**.

Peñabón

'**Peñabón**' or '**Peña de los Papos**' (depending on the map) is the mammoth lump of rock looming over **Trevélez**. This route tackles the higher of the two **Peñabón** peaks (2536 metres), from where you have superb views in all directions.

The **Cortijo de las Rosas** (Wp.6) is a good spot for bird watchers: we saw dozens of brilliantly coloured bee-catchers gliding, spinning and diving above the rocks. Other walkers have reported seeing golden eagles from the peak.

The optional descent to **Bérchules** is an easy if somewhat monotonous route mainly along dirt tracks. It provides an alternative to the **GR7** for linking villages and might also be useful for those staying in **Bérchules**, taking the morning bus to **Trevélez** and returning to **Bérchules** on foot. You'd have to be an early riser though - the morning bus leaves at 5.05am! Note, as a descent it is tolerable, but don't do it in reverse. It's a long drag up and the combination of climbing and monotony may well prove fatal. If you want to return to **Trevélez** from **Bérchules**, remember the evening bus also leaves at five. If you miss the bus, 'Barbero' provides a taxi service. Ask in the new houses on the right after the *fuente* as you descend toward the main road (gr-421).

* the walking is easy, but you do climb 1100 metres in a little over 4km and this is one of those Russian doll walks where you keep thinking you're there only to find yet another gruelling climb lurking behind the last one)
** **Trevélez-Peñabón** 3 hours (one-way), **Peñabón-Bérchules** 2¼ hours (one-way)
*** **Trevélez-Peñabón** 4.3km (one-way),**Peñabón-Bérchules** 7km
**** in **Trevélez** & **Bérchules**)

Short Version
It's worth climbing to **Wp.6** below the **Cortijo de las Rosas** for the views.

Buses back: **Bérchules** - **Trevélez** 5.05pm **Trevélez** - **Bérchules** 3.15pm / 8.30pm

From **Trevélez**, we follow the **GR7**/Walk 5 to the **Acequia de Cástaras** (Wp.2 10M), where we bear right. After 150 metres, we leave the **GR7** to take a clear path (green-white waymarks) climbing to the left (Wp.3 15M), bearing right at the Y-junction immediately afterwards. As the path approaches a large

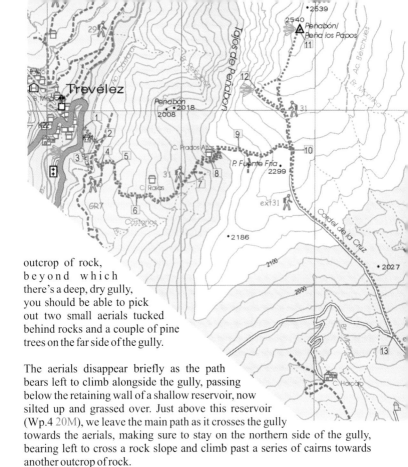

outcrop of rock,
beyond which
there's a deep, dry gully,
you should be able to pick
out two small aerials tucked
behind rocks and a couple of pine
trees on the far side of the gully.

The aerials disappear briefly as the path
bears left to climb alongside the gully, passing
below the retaining wall of a shallow reservoir, now
silted up and grassed over. Just above this reservoir
(Wp.4 20M), we leave the main path as it crosses the gully
towards the aerials, making sure to stay on the northern side of the gully,
bearing left to cross a rock slope and climb past a series of cairns towards
another outcrop of rock.

Just below the outcrop of rock, the 'path' (which is virtually invisible on the
rock slope) crosses the remains of an old wire gate then becomes clearer as it
winds up through the rocks. It then crosses the gully (Wp.5 26M) between a
couple of eglantine bushes before climbing steadily (S), eventually winding
into a pinewood a couple of hundred metres above the aerials.

The path emerges from the wood very briefly then continues climbing
between the trees along a route that is sometimes faint but always well-
marked with cairns, finally coming out at the wood's western limit (Wp.6
45M) within sight of the white **Cortijo de las Rosas**. We bear right along the
upper limit of the wood to a small rocky platform above the **Barranco de los
Castaños** then turn left to climb towards the *cortijo* along a faint path marked
by occasional cairns.

Leaving the *cortijo* on our left, we follow the path along the fence up to a small
reservoir, beyond which another pinewood begins. We take the faint path
climbing north-east between the pinewood and the **Barranco de los
Castaños**. When the path splinters into a series of goat tracks, we maintain
direction and climb steadily, following the main traces as they approach the

pinewood again a few minutes later. We stay just to the right of the pinewood until we reach a Y-junction near their upper limit (Wp.7 89M) where we bear left.

A hundred metres later, at the pinewood's westernmost tip, we turn right as the path zigzags up to the ruined **Cortijo de Prados Altos** (Wp.8 100M). After the ruin, the path occasionally loses definition, so keep your eye open for cairns and stick to the main traces as they wind up to a weedy reservoir (Wp.9 121M) near the head of the *barranco*.

After crossing a fence beyond the reservoir, we leave the main path as it bears south and climb alongside the watershed through the last stand of pine.

When the path disappears, we head north-east, away from watershed, and follow the cairns through the remaining pine and scrub up to the flat ridge above **Fuente Fría** where we join the traces of an old dirt track (Wp.10 140M).

Peñabón, seen from the south-west

We follow the dirt track north, ignoring a branch to the left (our return route), until it gradually gets fainter and finally disappears altogether. We then continue climbing across scrub and scree to pick up a clear path leading behind the first outcrop of rocks, after which we follow the ridge past two more outcrops until we reach the tall triangulation post marking the

Peñabón/Peña de los Papos peak (Wp.11 181M) where there's a tiny but sturdy and very welcome windbreak.

For a slightly different route back to Wp.10, we stay on the path after the first outcrop of rocks and, when it disappears, continue SW to join the left-hand branch of the track along the ridge which leads to a small pen (Wp.12 194M) for capturing *cabra montés*, behind which there are fine views across the **Tajos del Peñabón**. We then follow the dirt track back to Wp.10, from where we can either return to **Trevélez** by the same route or descend to **Bérchules** via the **Cordel de la Cruz de Bérchules**.

To descend to Bérchules
For Bérchules, we follow the dirt track (S) over a small hump, after which it dips down, running into a clear logging track alongside a firebreak. After a monotonous but easy descent (easy on everything but the knees), the logging track merges with the track for the **Cortijo El Horcajo** (Wp.13 238M), a potential way down to **Juviles** but unfortunately a 'permanent firing range'!

We bear left as the logging track, now better stabilised and less steep, leaves the firebreak and cuts through a pine forest, passing an open stretch above beehives before crossing more pine forest and joining **PF5** (Wp.14 249M). We follow **PF5** to the right for 500 metres and, just after the **Cortijo de Hoya Herrera**, bear left onto a rough dirt track (Wp.15 260M) descending past another pinewood towards several stands of beehives.

Immediately before the junction with another smoother dirt track (Wp.16 276M), we take the shortcut path on the left to join the track lower down above the dry **Barranco de Cairo**. Following the track round the head of the *barranco*, we turn right at the Y-junction. Just after a large inhabited *cortijo*, we leave the dirt track and take a narrow dirt path (Wp.17 285M) between the track and the *barranco*.

The path soon bears away from the *barranco* above a cherry orchard, before crossing another dirt track and descending towards a chestnut wood and an *acequia*. Bearing left, we follow the *acequia* path for ten metres before crossing the water channel and descending through more chestnut trees towards **Bérchules**, the first glimpses of which are visible through the trees. A steep descent along an old mule trail between fields leads to the outskirts of **Bérchules** next to a small *fuente* (Wp.18 305M) after which it's a ten minute descent to the centre of the village.

32 CERRO MACILLA CÁSTARAS

The **Barranco de Fuente Medina** is an enchanting little valley, leading down to the pretty village of **Cástaras**. Better still, nobody seems to know about it and the paths are all but deserted, unused except by the occasional shepherd and, if the spoors are anything to go by, the odd wild boar. However, being off the beaten track does have its drawbacks. Many paths dwindle into nothing while others have become so embrambled they're impassable. If you go exploring, be prepared to turn back. Wps. 8, 10, 12 & 14 are not on the map.

*   pan-handle circular
**   in **Cástaras** with luck, though the main **Bar Maria** is also mainly shut

Stroll
Cástaras - Barrancos de Alberquilla & Fuente Medina (Wps.8-14 & 6-8)

Access by car: To reach the start of the walk, take the dirt track (watch out for the erosion channels) on the left 1.3km from the western limit of **Juviles**. After 600 metres, park on the flat ground between the rocks of **Cerro Macilla** and the almond groves (Wp.1 0M).

On the western edge of the parking area, we take the old *acequia* path to the left of the almond grove. We follow this path as it bears left through *retama* before descending into the **Barranco de Fuente Medina**, where we bear right at a Y-junction (Wp.2 5M) just before the stream to cross both the stream and, five metres later, an old *acequia*.

After passing a large abandoned reservoir, the path continues alongside a series of terraces, gradually descending to re-cross the *acequia* and veer back toward the poplar lined stream. Ignoring a branch on the right (Wp.3 11M), we carry straight on, squeezing through a tunnel of *retama* to join a partially rock-laid path, crossing back onto the left bank of the now dry watercourse (Wp.4 16M) amid a stand of poplars.

A clearer path marked by a white cross (not a waymark) follows the left bank down to a more densely wooded stretch of young poplars where the water re-emerges from an underground source. We continue descending, crossing another *acequia* before re-crossing the stream next to a small waterfall (Wp.5 30M).

After a brief climb along the right bank, the path passes a series of clear grassy terraces before returning to the riverbed beside a large reservoir, a little way below which the three spouts of the **Fuente Solís** (Wp.6 40M) nestle below a large overhanging rock.

Fuente Solís

The cobbled path

We continue along the right bank on a more closely cobbled stretch which soon goes to the right of a large, partially restored house, before descending to join the main track from the house down past a white water hut with a blue door to a T-junction (Wp.7 50M).

If coming from Cástaras
- the Wp.7 junction is the second path on the right after the first houses above the road.

To continue to the village
We turn left and descend a concreted alley-cum-track joining the road (Wp.8 59M) just west of **Cástaras**.

N.B. If you're starting from **Cástaras**, this track is the one just before the '40km for 1.5km' speed limit sign; it's signposted 'Casa Sabrina' and 'Las Vigilias'.

If you don't wish to visit the village
Turn right at **Wp.7** for a steady climb to a ruin and junction of paths (Wp.9 73M) on the edge of what appears to be a discrete hamlet, but is in fact the largely abandoned **Barrio Alto de Cástaras**.

After taking the left-hand branch into the 'hamlet', we bear right on the path climbing behind the first house to a broader cobbled track next to a *fuente* (Wp.10 75M) where the real climb into the **Barranco de Alberquillas** begins. Ignoring a branch on the left (Wp.11 77M), we continue climbing toward the poplar topped rocks behind the hamlet, where there's a small *cortijo* with breeze block outbuildings (Wp.12 84M) and, behind it, a small *acequia*.

We follow the *acequia*, ignoring a branch up to a manmade waterfall, and climb steadily to the head of the *barranco* where there's a large reservoir (Wp.13 90M). Ignoring the main trail climbing to the left, we take the path bearing right behind the reservoir. After a brief climb, the path levels out before bearing left to a small col above an almond grove, from which a mule trail zigzags back into the **Barranco de Fuente Medina**, rejoining the outward route (Wp.14 105M) about thirty minutes below **Cerro Macilla**.

An outstanding walk, following an exceptionally pretty *acequia* and returning along a mule trail with splendid views of the valley. There's one stretch of the *acequia* along a narrow wall above a small drop and another traversing a badly eroded slope, but otherwise the walking is easy. If your vertigo is really acute, you may wish to skip the *acequia* and take the return route both ways (see Wp.10). The extension, an attractive walk in its own right, is specially recommended if you want to do Walk 34. The alternative route back from the extension requires slightly better path finding skills. Wp.5 is not marked on the map. Park in the main car-park next to the track down to the **Fuente Agria de Bérchules**.

As with many walks from the first edition of this book, this route has acquired quasi-official status and a version of the itinerary, focusing on our alternative return, has been marked with PR-style wayposts. Two other 'new' routes, one of which partially mirrorsg a stretch of our

New and old signs en route

Walk 7, are sketched on a mapboard in front of **Fuente Carmelas** on the way to the village.

| 3 🚶 | ⌚ 2H 5M * | ➡ 6 km | ** ⛰ | ↗ 200m *** ↘ 200m | 🔄 | 🍴 5 **** |

* For the extension add 1 hour 40 minutes (incl. return)
** + 4 km for the extension
*** 470m with the extension
**** in **Bérchules**

Stroll
Acequia Nueva. Bear right at Wp.2 (the main junction after the large chestnut tree, not the minor junction next to the telegraph poles) descend to the *acequia* and follow it back to a little bridge onto the horseshoe threshing circle, from where we can rejoin the main path back into **Bérchules**.

From **Bar Los Vergeles** in **Bérchules** church square we take **Calle Iglesia** (N) and then cross **Plaza Arastos** to follow **Calle Real** to a triple-junction, continuing straight ahead on **Calle García**. We bear right twenty metres later onto a concrete lane up to a *fuente/lavadero* and a broad dirt path signposted for the **Junta de los Ríos** (Wp.10M).

The path runs alongside apple and pear orchards, crossing a watercourse just above a roofless mill before climbing behind a large horseshoe-shaped threshing circle, from where the **Loma de Enmedio** above the **Ríos Chico** and **Grande** is visible. After passing a second threshing circle, the old path is engulfed by a new dirt track.

Acequia Nueva

Ignoring a branch on the right fifty metres after the second threshing circle (Wp.2 10M), we bear left to follow the main track. Immediately after an access track into another orchard, we leave the new dirt track, and bear right to rejoin the old path (Wp.3 13M) above a small reservoir protected by a sloping wire fence supported by corroded metal posts. Five metres after the flat-roofed house abutting onto the reservoir, we bear right again to join the path along the **Acequia Nueva**. The *acequia* is a delight, flanked by chestnut, walnut, mulberry, blackberry, clover and mint, and lined with clumps of a curious pink weed.

Despite occasionally going underground and passing stretches lined or walled with PVC, corrugated-iron and sheet-metal, it maintains its charm. We now follow the *acequero*'s path all the way to the **Junta de los Ríos**.

Notes:
(a) After a brief stretch where the water is piped underground, the path bears left and climbs slightly to run along a narrow wall for ten metres above a three-metre drop.
(b) After passing a couple of bedstead gates, a branch to the right (Wp.4 35M) leads onto a natural *mirador*.
(c) After the landscape becomes more barren, there's a slightly tricky stretch (Wp.5 59M) where the water is piped underground and we have to scramble along an eroded slope.

Almost immediately after Wp.5, another path comes in from the left (Wp.6). This is the return route. For now, we bear right and continue along the *acequia* for 5 minutes to the **Junta de los Ríos**, where we cross the **Río Chico** bridge and reach the **Fábrica de Moros** ruins below the **Tajos de Reyecillo** or **Reyezuelo**, last refuge of the leaders of the 1568 Moorish rebellion (64M).

For the extension
We take the broad mule-track climbing to the left of the **Fábrica de Moros** ruins. A succession of three easy climbs with fine views of the **Tajos de Reyecillo** (you may spot a sizeable herd of wild boar with their babies here in spring) leads to a Y-junction (Wp.7 33M).

Bearing right onto a narrower path, we pass two *cortijos*, the first inhabited in the summer, the second ruined and facing three other roofless ruins on the eastern side of the river. The path gradually descends to the river, getting narrower and more overgrown, and passing several muddy stretches, before fording the **Río Grande** (Wp.8 52M) into a large stand of poplars, visible since the ruined *cortijo*.

For an alternative return to the Junta de los Ríos,
We hop over the rough barbed-wire fence ten metres before the ford and cross the meadow down to the river. We then follow the cow paths for the next fifteen minutes, crossing and re-crossing the river, aiming first for two large bushy poplars, then for a stone hut on a promontory on the left bank above the river (the lower of the three ruins mentioned above).

Just before the promontory, we bear right to cross the river yet again and pick up a more clearly traced cow path that almost immediately re-crosses the river! Ignoring the branch climbing to the right (my apologies, but the logic of a cow is a sorry thing) we cross back onto the right bank to follow the path as it climbs above the river (S).

Ignoring another minor branch after fifteen metres, we stick to the main traces, climbing gently to cross the eroded flank of a field. We then bear left at a Y-junction and pass behind the ruins of a small byre (Wp.9 81M) where the path disappears. Maintaining altitude, we continue SW towards a stretch of fencing and two small, half-dead walnut trees, thirty metres after which we rejoin the main mule track (86M) fifteen minutes from the **Junta de los Ríos**.

From the **Junta de los Ríos**, it's five minutes down to the junction of paths at Wp.6. Crossing the watercourse feeding into the **Acequia Nueva**, we follow the path up to a *cortijo*/threshing circle, where it broadens to a mule track, following the contours of the mountain to emerge on a branch of the new dirt track (Wp.10 forty minutes from the **Junta de los Ríos**) which we join one hundred metres later. We bear left and follow the dirt track back to Wp.3 to arrive back in **Bérchules** one hour from the **Junta de los Ríos**.

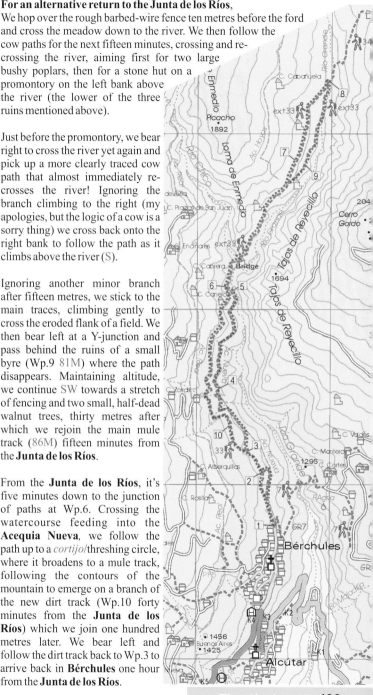

A simple if slightly tame ascent, but the views on the way up are good and, from the top, excellent, while the descent along the **Río Grande** and the **Acequia Nueva** (Walk 33) is one of the most attractive routes in the region. Park as per Walk 33.

| 4 | 5¾ H | 15 km | 880m / 880m | ↻ | 5* |

Stroll
See **Pista Forestal 5**

* in **Bérchules**

From **Bérchules** church (Wp.1 0M) follow **GR7**/Walk 7 Wps. 8-11 to the dirt track (Wp.2 59M). NOTE: the rocky outcrop visible above the **Cortijos Cortes** and **Montero** on the far side of the river is the **Cima de Tejar** (Wp.5).

Turning left on the dirt track, we pass a puzzling 'GR7' waypost (according to the maps, it shouldn't be there!) and follow the track till it bears right at the **Cortijo Montero**. We can stay on the dirt track here, but it's quicker to go behind the **Montero** chapel and climb the slope (E) directly behind the *cortijo* (Wp.3 75M) to rejoin the track one hundred metres later.

We then follow the dirt track above a huge concrete reservoir and, 250 metres after a U-bend, bear right on a very rough, very steep maintenance track (Wp.4 91M) up to the fence below the **Tejar** pinewood.

We follow this track (N) alongside the fence to join another track, where we turn right, to cross the fence and climb (E) to the wide firebreak (Wp.5 110M) behind the **Cima de Tejar**. To the north, you might be able to pick out the flash of a white flag beside **Cerro Gordo** firewatch hut and, to the south, on a clear day, Africa.

Montero and Cima de Tejar

From the **Cima de Tejar**, we take the dirt track up the firebreak (N). After passing a first branch on the left twenty minutes later, the track gradually levels out before a second branch on the left (Wp.6 148M) climbs to **Cerro Gordo**. We can either follow the dirt track all the way to the top or, when it turns sharp right and we see the **Mulhacén** and **Alcazaba** to the west, climb off-path directly to the firewatch hut (Wp.7 169M). From the firewatch hut, we follow a faint logging track (N) until it peters out on a grassy platform above the **Cerro Gordo** crags.

N.B. From here it's worthwhile tracing an imaginary line down from the white-walled reservoir on the eastern side of the valley to pinpoint the stand of poplars at Wp.12.

Looking north from below the summit

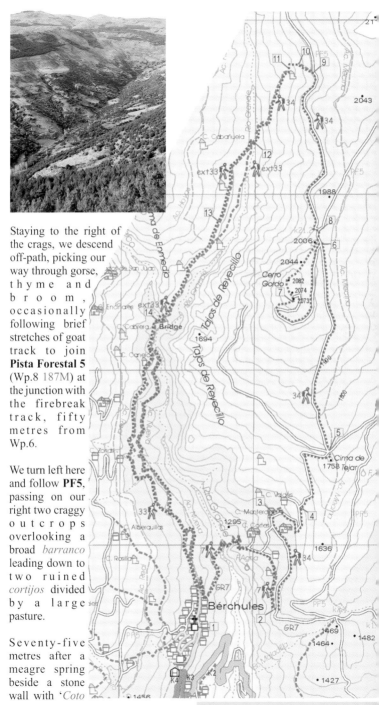

Staying to the right of the crags, we descend off-path, picking our way through gorse, t h y m e a n d b r o o m , occasionally following brief stretches of goat track to join **Pista Forestal 5** (Wp.8 187M) at the junction with the firebreak track, fifty metres from Wp.6.

We turn left here and follow **PF5**, passing on our right two craggy o u t c r o p s overlooking a broad *barranco* leading down to t w o r u i n e d *cortijos* divided b y a l a r g e pasture.

S e v e n t y - f i v e metres after a meagre spring beside a stone wall with 'Coto

Privado' daubed on it in large white letters and topped with a '*Parque Nacional*' sign, we turn left at a large cairn (Wp.9 216M) to take the very faint remains of an ancient cow path (so faint and ancient it is, to all intents and purposes, 'off-path') zigzagging down to the first ruin.

The 'path' winds down twenty metres, then bears right and descends to a watercourse. We follow the left bank of the watercourse down to a slightly damp stretch then cross onto the northern side, where an irrigation canal channelled with slates marks the top of a shaley slope (Wp.10 221M) descending to the first ruin. We follow a very faint 'path' across the slope then bear left for a rough, steep descent to a clear path just above the ruin (Wp.11 227M).

A reasonably clear path in front of the ruin's threshing circle, re-crosses the watercourse then bears away from it and gradually descends through an oak forest (SSW). When the path emerges from the forest, we bear right across a small field then follow the river for 150 metres to the large stand of poplars (Wp.12 245M), halfway along which a ford crosses the river (Wp.8 of Walk 33).

From here, we can either take the alternative descent described in Walk 33, or stay on the principal path for a gentle climb to the main mule trail (Wp.13 265M) down to the **Junta de los Ríos** (Wp.14 285M).

After crossing the bridge over the **Río Chico** we follow the **Acequia Nueva** for a couple of hundred metres to a path climbing off to the right (Wp.6 of Walk 33), where we again have a choice of routes, either following Walk 33 down to **Bérchules** or, recommended, bearing left to continue along the *acequia* (see Walk 33 for a generic description) until it joins the new dirt track (Wp.3 of Walk 33) above **Bérchules**.

When the dirt track comes to a fence next to a threshing circle, we bear right on a narrow path leading into **Bérchules** (one hour from Wp.14) at the top of **Calle Garcia** which leads to **Calle Real** and Plaza **Arastos**.

Waymarking on the **PR111** is surreal, deftly blending abundance with obscurity, the one when paint is perfectly superfluous, the other when a waypost is most vital, but one shouldn't hold window dressing against such a wonderful walk. The **Acequia de los Castaños** is one of the finest man-made waterways in the Alpujarras and a must for any devotee of woodland walking and *acequias*. Especially recommended in autumn, but a great walk in any season.

| 2 | 1¾ H * | 6.75 km | 175m / 175m | ↻ | 4 |

* I can only suppose the official time (4 hours) anticipates getting badly lost around the Wp.8 mark. That said, there's so much to linger over, you should allow up to 3 hours for really enjoying the walk.

Alternative, easier version
Continue along the *acequia* at Wp.4 and again at Wp.9 to its source in the **Río Mecina** 900 metres later. Return via the same route.

Access on foot: from **Mecina-Bombaron**

Access by car: take the concrete track from the western limit of **Mecina-Bombarón** up to **Calle Plaza Vieja** and park in the **Plaza Vieja** itself.

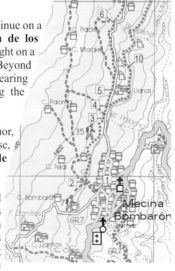

From the *plaza*, take the narrow street climbing beside the *fuente* (signposted 'Bérchules 2h') and bear right onto **Calle Castillo** (signposted 'Sendero de las Acequias 4h') (Wp.1 0M).

From the top of **Calle Castillo**, we continue on a mule trail till it crosses the **Acequia de los Castaños** (Wp.2 3M), where we bear right on a minor path passing a large reservoir. Beyond the reservoir, we follow a narrow path bearing away from the main *acequia* feeding the reservoir.

We then climb slightly alongside a minor, dry *acequia*, passing above a small house, behind which we rejoin the **Acequia de los Castaños**.

The *acequia* path soon runs into a broad trail (an alternative, waymarked access from the village) (Wp.3 13M), which shadows the channel for 125-metres then forks left (Wp.4), rapidly becoming a partially cobbled trail climbing to join a dirt track (Wp.5 18M).

The Acequia de los Castaños

We now simply follow this track to the north through a delightfully bucolic landscape peppered with well-maintained *cortijos* and enticing country cabins enjoying great views up toward the head of the **Río Mecina**.

After a gentle climb, we reach a major, waymarked Y-junction, where we fork right, away from the 'Propiedad Privada' track (Wp.6 28M), and dip down briefly. We stick with the main track until oak begin to mingle among the chestnut and poplar, and we come to another major waymarked junction, where we again fork right (Wp.7 46M).

Our branch track descends past twin threshing circles, a small cabin and ancient threshing machine, after which we leave the track, forking right on a broad trail descending to a crumbling *cortijo* with large waymarks on the corner of the main building (Wp.8 50M).

The onward route is not immediately obvious, but descending to the right of the *cortijo* then immediately bearing left along its lower edge (WITHOUT descending into the gully below it), we recover a minor track at the eastern end of the *cortijo*, which descends past a PVC-lined reservoir and a small cabin to rejoin the **Acequia de los Castaños** (Wp.9 56M).

Descending back to the *acequia*

Having negotiated the *cortijo* descent, pathfinding problems disappear, as we now simply turn right and follow the *acequia*, crossing a dirt track leading to a *cortijo* that lies below the *acequia* (Wp.10 75M) before rejoining our outward route at Wp.4 (87M). We can either bear left at Wp.3 and follow the broad trail back to the village then bear right and keep bearing right round the outskirts of the village to return to the **Plaza Vieja** or (more direct and more attractive) follow the outward leg along the *acequia* back to the start.

See the notes on Using GPS in the Alpujarras on page 19.

1
Lanjarón - Cáñar - Soportújar

Wp		Latitude		Longitude
1	36	55.1645	3	28.2192
2	36	55.0919	3	28.1243
3	36	55.1363	3	28.0175
4	36	55.1843	3	27.9125
5	36	55.1837	3	27.7343
6	36	55.0376	3	27.5491
7	36	55.0691	3	27.1901
8	36	55.2384	3	26.7707
9	36	55.2804	3	26.6777
10	36	55.3260	3	26.6375
11	36	55.5732	3	26.5145
12	36	55.6350	3	26.5055
13	36	55.8648	3	26.4347
14	36	55.7148	3	26.2051
15	36	55.6962	3	25.9303
16	36	55.5948	3	25.7359
17	36	55.5858	3	25.5433
18	36	56.3034	3	24.8587
19	36	56.4684	3	24.7225
20	36	56.3670	3	24.6649
21	36	55.9428	3	24.5724
22	36	55.8594	3	24.5184
23	36	55.7892	3	24.4734
24	36	55.7250	3	24.4188
25	36	55.4736	3	24.4830
26	36	55.2462	3	24.7272

2
Soportújar - Pampaneira

Wp		Latitude		Longitude
1	36	55.5780	3	23.9250
2	36	55.5300	3	23.5224
3	36	55.5570	3	23.4084
4	36	55.4352	3	23.2392
5	36	55.4676	3	23.1144
6	36	55.6482	3	22.6938
7	36	55.9332	3	22.4898
8	36	56.3113	3	22.0224
9	36	56.5405	3	21.8316
10	36	56.5129	3	21.7002

3
Bubión - Pitres

Wp		Latitude		Longitude
1	36	56.8633	3	21.2346
2	36	56.6065	3	21.1392
3	36	56.4367	3	21.0846
4	36	56.3905	3	20.9898
5	36	56.3173	3	20.7900
6	36	56.4209	3	20.1797
7	36	56.3753	3	20.0699
8	36	56.4053	3	19.7927
9	36	56.2320	3	19.6524
10	36	56.5608	3	19.8426

4
Busquístar - Trevélez

Wp		Latitude		Longitude
1	36	56.3250	3	17.6778
2	36	56.3886	3	17.4708
3	36	56.4894	3	17.3982
4	36	57.0264	3	17.2482
5	36	57.0696	3	17.1588
6	36	57.4158	3	17.4510
7	36	57.8322	3	17.2152
8	36	57.9966	3	17.3964
9	36	58.5714	3	17.1294
10	36	58.9770	3	17.2740
11	36	59.1918	3	17.3982
12	36	59.2308	3	17.1978
13	36	59.1720	3	16.8732
14	36	59.2740	3	16.8996
15	36	59.6220	3	16.4868
16	36	59.9370	3	16.4022
17	37	00.0948	3	16.3920
18	37	00.2148	3	16.2270

5
Trevélez - Juviles

Wp		Latitude		Longitude
1	36	59.9605	3	15.7495
2	36	59.8465	3	15.6289
3	36	59.5003	3	15.7555
4	36	59.3173	3	15.7015
5	36	58.4934	3	15.6444
6	36	58.1496	3	15.5490
7	36	57.7440	3	15.3258
8	36	57.7146	3	15.2274
9	36	57.6960	3	14.9238
10	36	57.3150	3	13.8432
11	36	57.1752	3	13.5942
12	36	56.9112	3	13.5323

6
Juviles - Cádiar - Lobras

Wp		Latitude		Longitude
1	36	56.9934	3	13.4435
2	36	57.0265	3	13.0109
3	36	56.8849	3	12.6767
4	36	56.7073	3	12.6395
5	36	56.4480	3	12.9533
6	36	56.2284	3	13.0045
7	36	55.9680	3	12.8809
8	36	55.8690	3	12.8701
9	36	55.5108	3	12.6805
10	36	55.5036	3	12.3690
11	36	55.5786	3	12.0048
12	36	55.5654	3	11.6892
13	36	55.6242	3	11.4948
14	36	55.7833	3	11.1948
15	36	56.3743	3	10.8564
16	36	56.7283	3	10.9266
17	36	55.8211	3	10.6878
18	36	55.7059	3	10.6566
19	36	55.4220	3	10.9938
20	36	55.1844	3	11.6154
21	36	55.0032	3	12.0018
22	36	54.9090	3	12.3330
23	36	54.8094	3	12.5502
24	36	54.8586	3	12.7134
25	36	55.8516	3	12.4273
26	36	55.8276	3	12.7525

7
Cádiar - Mecina Bombarón

Wp		Latitude		Longitude
1	36	56.6341	3	10.8168
2	36	56.8327	3	10.9296
3	36	57.3557	3	10.8151
4	36	57.4511	3	10.8247
5	36	57.6563	3	11.2723
6	36	57.6917	3	11.4085
7	36	57.9041	3	11.4461
8	36	58.7075	3	11.3951
9	36	59.0472	3	11.2589
10	36	58.9716	3	10.9667
11	36	58.6638	3	10.8359
12	36	58.6056	3	10.4383
13	36	58.9230	3	09.4669

8
Lobras - Busquístar

Wp		Latitude		Longitude
1	36	55.6146	3	12.7039
2	36	55.4004	3	13.5451
3	36	55.4856	3	13.7525
4	36	55.8552	3	13.6631
5	36	56.0022	3	13.8521
6	36	55.9038	3	15.2124
7	36	55.7724	3	15.5346
8	36	55.2696	3	15.8424
9	36	54.9767	3	16.5906
10	36	55.5312	3	17.0664
11	36	55.6152	3	17.2818
12	36	55.9392	3	17.4096
13	36	56.1900	3	17.6562

9

Órgiva - Lanjarón

Wp	Latitude		Longitude
1	36	54.1542	3 25.5648
2	36	54.1235	3 25.6938
3	36	54.2117	3 25.9050
4	36	54.2975	3 26.0442
5	36	54.7572	3 26.1739
6	36	54.8742	3 26.5477
7	36	54.9420	3 26.6461
8	36	54.9737	3 26.9617
9	36	55.0427	3 27.2009
10	36	54.9671	3 27.6137
11	36	54.9983	3 27.9113
12	36	54.8711	3 28.2671
13	36	55.1417	3 28.2210

10

El Caballo

Wp	Latitude		Longitude
1	36	58.5162	3 27.8532
2	36	58.8576	3 27.8706
3	36	59.3838	3 27.5664
4	37	00.1596	3 26.7798
5	37	00.4092	3 26.4954
6	37	00.7182	3 26.3844
7	37	00.8562	3 26.2266
8	37	00.3510	3 26.7378
9	37	00.1152	3 26.9172
10	36	59.3766	3 27.4722
11	36	58.9782	3 27.8052

11

Cerro Man - Puente Palo

Wp	Latitude		Longitude
1	36	56.4546	3 25.4646
2	36	56.5674	3 25.5120
3	36	56.7696	3 25.5414
4	36	57.1548	3 25.5090
5	36	57.2418	3 25.4496
6	36	57.4842	3 25.1364
7	36	57.8340	3 24.9486
8	36	57.9720	3 24.7968
9	36	57.3150	3 25.4178

12

Prado Grande - Puente Palo - Prado Grande

Wp	Latitude		Longitude
1	36	56.5410	3 24.3498
2	36	56.9088	3 24.3810
3	36	57.0948	3 24.6084
4	36	57.2046	3 24.6294
5	36	57.3738	3 24.5448
6	36	57.7104	3 24.4992
7	36	57.9330	3 24.4662
8	36	58.1286	3 24.5436

13

Puente Palo - Pico de Alegas - Puente Palo

Wp	Latitude		Longitude
01	36	58.0165	3 24.7859
02	36	58.3927	3 24.6929
03	36	58.5061	3 24.8645
4	36	59.1509	3 24.2850
5	36	59.3801	3 24.1806
6	36	59.3027	3 24.1416
7	36	59.2541	3 24.1079
8	36	59.2793	3 24.1043
9	36	59.3231	3 24.1019
10	36	59.2577	3 24.0653
11	36	59.3453	3 24.0509
12	36	59.4155	3 24.0197
13	36	59.4707	3 23.9591
14	36	59.4791	3 23.9081
15	36	59.3843	3 23.9207
16	36	59.6075	3 23.8343
17	36	59.8805	3 23.5487
18	37	00.0786	3 23.5116
19	36	58.9631	3 23.7623
20	36	58.1569	3 23.6281
21	36	57.7993	3 23.6239
22	36	57.9505	3 24.4691

14

Loma de Cáñar

Wp	Latitude		Longitude
1	36	58.0170	3 24.7908
2	36	58.5054	3 24.8664
3	36	58.4532	3 25.1562
4	36	58.8966	3 24.9756
5	36	59.0670	3 25.0338
6	36	59.1048	3 25.0734
7	36	59.3976	3 25.2510
8	36	59.7174	3 25.2252
9	36	59.2056	3 25.6698
10	36	58.8102	3 25.9116
11	36	58.6872	3 25.9134
12	36	58.6260	3 25.8390
13	36	58.6704	3 25.7412
14	36	58.4898	3 25.7238
15	36	57.8430	3 25.8498
16	36	57.3240	3 25.4154

15

Poqueira Villages.

Wp	Latitude		Longitude
1	36	56.4630	3 21.5904
2	36	56.5572	3 21.5586
3	36	56.5824	3 21.4776
4	36	56.8764	3 21.4158
5	36	57.0450	3 21.4944
6	36	57.2724	3 21.5430
7	36	57.4170	3 21.8574
8	36	57.4410	3 21.9648
9	36	57.5670	3 21.9558
10	36	57.5934	3 21.9816
11	36	57.6858	3 22.1082
12	36	58.0134	3 21.8886
13	36	58.0566	3 21.7764
14	36	57.7284	3 21.6726
15	36	57.6612	3 21.7332
16	36	57.0240	3 22.0626
17	36	56.8098	3 21.8760
18	36	56.8344	3 21.7596

16

Pampaneira - Pitres - Pampaneira

Wp	Latitude		Longitude
1	36	56.3172	3 21.6060
2	36	56.4282	3 21.5028
3	36	56.4336	3 21.3564
4	36	56.4198	3 21.3042
5	36	56.4498	3 21.2880
6	36	56.4102	3 21.1032
7	36	56.3700	3 21.0078
8	36	56.6238	3 20.8350
9	36	56.2668	3 20.3760
10	36	56.0064	3 20.7966
11	36	56.0190	3 20.4648
12	36	56.0052	3 20.3586
13	36	56.1570	3 20.0292
14	36	56.1468	3 19.8894
15	36	56.1678	3 19.6008
16	36	56.0280	3 21.1632
17	36	55.9566	3 21.2460
18	36	55.8828	3 21.2598
19	36	55.8546	3 21.3378
20	36	55.7766	3 21.6942
21	36	55.8984	3 21.2040

17

Capileira - La Cebadilla - Capileira

Wp	Latitude		Longitude
1	36	57.7295	3 21.5694
2	36	57.9185	3 21.5190
3	36	57.9905	3 21.4518
4	36	58.2095	3 21.3522
5	36	58.6206	3 21.3138
6	36	59.3766	3 21.0492
7	36	59.1588	3 21.2754
8	36	58.9548	3 21.5088
9	36	58.1795	3 21.7734
10	36	57.8081	3 21.6444

18

Río Naute Circuit.

Wp	Latitude		Longitude
01	36	59.3808	3 21.0480
02	36	59.6292	3 20.9946
03	36	59.6784	3 20.9940
04	36	59.8458	3 20.9202
05	37	00.2418	3 20.5104
06	37	00.3012	3 20.4210
08	37	00.7386	3 20.1660

19

Toril Valley Acequias

Wp	Latitude	Longitude
09	37 00.9576	3 20.1330
10	37 00.9942	3 20.1858
11	37 01.0662	3 20.2344
12	37 01.1520	3 20.6244
13	37 00.7986	3 20.5560
14	37 00.7440	3 20.6838
15	37 00.4656	3 21.2094
16	36 59.8038	3 21.0618
1	36 59.3832	3 21.0486
2	36 59.1660	3 21.2670
3	36 59.2956	3 21.3846
4	36 59.4738	3 21.4122
5	36 59.6604	3 21.5892
6	37 00.2922	3 22.1268
7	37 00.6522	3 22.3188
8	37 00.7596	3 22.5864
9	37 00.6684	3 22.9626
10	37 00.2484	3 22.5036
11	36 59.6382	3 22.1694
12	36 59.4840	3 21.5250

20

O.Sel.Ling

Wp	Latitude	Longitude
01	36 57.4446	3 21.9102
02	36 57.4332	3 21.9672
03	36 57.5424	3 21.9384
04	36 57.5958	3 21.9852
05	36 57.6762	3 22.1130
06	36 57.5994	3 22.2252
07	36 57.5538	3 22.3152
08	36 57.5898	3 22.3536
09	36 57.5850	3 22.4346
10	36 57.3204	3 22.4286
11	36 57.3774	3 22.6182
12	36 57.1104	3 22.7784
13	36 57.0960	3 22.9230
14	36 56.5680	3 23.0964
15	36 56.3694	3 23.1978
16	36 56.1732	3 23.2104
17	36 56.0712	3 23.0508
18	36 56.4852	3 22.6878
19	36 56.7882	3 22.4412
20	36 57.0708	3 22.2948
21	36 57.1128	3 22.1196
22	36 57.0234	3 22.0596

21

Poqueira Refuge

Wp	Latitude	Longitude
1	36 58.3536	3 20.6844
2	36 58.5630	3 20.5470
3	36 59.2482	3 20.2464
4	36 59.6310	3 20.1432
5	36 59.8866	3 19.9116
6	37 01.0836	3 19.8036
7	37 01.1616	3 19.6974
8	37 01.6501	3 19.4233
9	36 59.9154	3 19.8552
10	36 59.6562	3 20.0928
11	36 58.5606	3 20.4666
12	37 01.0032	3 19.8534
13	37 00.5784	3 19.9596
14	37 00.0312	3 19.9230
15	36 59.3718	3 20.2734
16	36 59.0688	3 20.4246

22

The Mulhacén from Hoya del Portillo

Wp	Latitude	Longitude
1	36 58.1476	3 20.0263
2	36 58.5372	3 19.9554
3	36 58.6596	3 19.8414
4	36 59.2764	3 19.6758
5	36 59.4522	3 19.4844
6	37 00.8454	3 18.6558
7	37 01.6494	3 19.4178
8	37 02.2446	3 19.5036
9	37 02.8176	3 19.4760
10	37 03.2520	3 19.4862
11	37 03.2868	3 19.5888
12	37 03.1470	3 19.0338
13	37 03.2064	3 18.6924
14	37 02.6580	3 18.7236
15	37 02.2182	3 18.2862
16	37 00.7932	3 18.2166
17	37 00.5556	3 18.1530
S1	37 00.5424	3 18.1602
S2	37 01.5354	3 18.4080
S3	37 03.1254	3 19.3170
S4	37 03.1602	3 19.2006

23

Pórtugos Junta de los Ríos

Wp	Latitude	Longitude
1	36 56.7336	3 19.1598
2	36 56.9202	3 19.1988
3	36 57.1920	3 19.3920
4	36 57.3132	3 19.5138
5	36 57.3558	3 19.5642
6	36 57.4410	3 19.6728
7	36 57.2082	3 19.8024
8	36 57.1308	3 19.7760
9	36 56.8458	3 19.4844
10	36 56.6436	3 19.4028
11	36 56.5176	3 19.5978
12	36 56.4804	3 19.3974
13	36 56.4504	3 19.2498
14	36 56.4174	3 18.9342

24

Tahá 1

Wp	Latitude	Longitude
1	36 56.2325	3 19.3789
2	36 56.2775	3 19.3027
3	36 56.2409	3 19.1347
4	36 56.0711	3 18.5155
5	36 56.1407	3 18.5263
6	36 56.4474	3 18.6762
7	36 56.2440	3 18.1548
8	36 56.3478	3 17.7810
9	36 56.1930	3 17.7192
10	36 55.8317	3 18.1188
11	36 55.8677	3 18.1938
12	36 56.1438	3 18.1326
13	36 56.0417	3 18.3492

25

Tahá 2

Wp	Latitude	Longitude
1	36 56.0526	3 18.6972
2	36 55.9098	3 18.7584
3	36 55.7232	3 18.8172
4	36 55.6758	3 19.1094
5	36 55.6140	3 19.1760
6	36 55.4928	3 19.0392
7	36 55.6566	3 18.9690
8	36 55.8462	3 18.5394
9	36 55.8270	3 18.4080
10	36 56.0244	3 18.5364
11	36 56.0244	3 18.6138

26

Sierra Mecina

Wp	Latitude	Longitude
1	36 55.5448	3 19.2965
2	36 54.9990	3 19.6176
3	36 54.7284	3 19.8666
4	36 55.2960	3 17.9166
5	36 55.5366	3 18.0552
6	36 55.6692	3 18.0414
7	36 55.8210	3 18.3720
8	36 55.8288	3 18.4080

27

Los Helechones, El Portichuelo de Cástaras & Los Cerillos Negros

Wp	Latitude	Longitude
1	36 56.2398	3 17.6040
2	36 56.4396	3 17.1336
3	36 56.6484	3 16.8702
4	36 56.7198	3 16.6596
5	36 56.8782	3 16.3386
6	36 56.9892	3 16.2366
7	36 56.6928	3 16.1694
8	36 56.5812	3 16.3158
9	36 56.4954	3 16.5738
10	36 56.2536	3 16.6368

28

Río Culo Perro

Wp	Latitude	Longitude
01	37 00.1758	3 15.9786
02	37 00.3918	3 16.0002

03	37	01.0764	3 15.6702
04	37	01.9002	3 15.3558
05	37	02.0202	3 15.3480
06	37	02.1216	3 15.3708
07	37	02.3310	3 15.4560
08	37	02.0160	3 15.1314
09	37	02.0844	3 14.8902
10	37	02.1282	3 14.9118
11	37	02.1354	3 14.7738

29
Headwaters of the Río Trevélez

Wp		Latitude	Longitude
1	37	00.0604	3 15.8792
2	37	00.3079	3 15.6503
3	37	00.9444	3 15.2700
4	37	01.3607	3 15.2177
5	37	01.4958	3 15.0899
6	37	01.8654	3 14.9369
7	37	02.1354	3 14.7749
8	37	02.7852	3 14.5386
9	37	03.2574	3 14.4942
10	37	03.7164	3 14.5572
11	37	03.8898	3 14.6142

30
Siete Lagunas + optional descent via Mirador de Trevélez

Wp		Latitude	Longitude
1	37	00.1789	3 15.9773
2	37	01.4291	3 15.9480
2A	37	01.0811	3 15.6703
3	37	01.9553	3 16.3230
4	37	02.4803	3 16.9662
5	37	02.8307	3 17.4048
6	37	02.8619	3 17.6238
7	37	02.7389	3 17.6142
8	37	02.4341	3 17.7408
9	37	02.1065	3 17.9964
10	37	00.5641	3 18.0870
11	37	00.4555	3 17.3748
12	37	00.2041	3 16.8311
13	37	00.2227	3 16.3661

31
Trevélez to Peñabon + optional descent to Bérchules

Wp		Latitude	Longitude
1	36	59.9671	3 15.7219
2	36	59.8201	3 15.6313
3	36	59.7673	3 15.6403
4	36	59.6851	3 15.6121
5	36	59.6989	3 15.5047
6	36	59.5206	3 15.3246
7	36	59.6580	3 14.8944
8	36	59.7335	3 14.7936
9	36	59.7893	3 14.5728
10	36	59.7899	3 14.1762
11	37	00.4721	3 14.1127
12	37	00.1157	3 14.4445
13	36	58.7201	3 13.4094
14	36	58.6505	3 13.1094
15	36	58.5209	3 12.8148
16	36	58.3733	3 12.3126
17	36	58.4021	3 12.1331
18	36	58.4045	3 11.6525

32
Cerro Macilla - Cástaras

Wp		Latitude	Longitude
1	36	56.6598	3 14.6310
2	36	56.5782	3 14.7780
3	36	56.5254	3 14.9160
4	36	56.4516	3 15.0012
5	36	56.2998	3 15.0984
6	36	56.1318	3 15.1866
7	36	55.9884	3 15.2682
8	36	55.9584	3 15.2796
9	36	56.0838	3 15.4140
10	36	56.0808	3 15.4746
11	36	56.1096	3 15.5304
12	36	56.1642	3 15.4728
13	36	56.3088	3 15.3804
14	36	56.2152	3 15.1548

33
Bérchules Junta de los Ríos

Wp		Latitude	Longitude
1	36	58.7580	3 11.4101
2	36	59.0694	3 11.4725
3	36	59.1678	3 11.5776
4	36	59.5332	3 11.8122
5	37	00.1254	3 11.7372
6	37	00.1422	3 11.7588
7	37	00.8304	3 11.2476
8	37	01.4118	3 11.0094
9	37	00.8118	3 11.1834
10	36	59.3166	3 11.7030

34
Bérchules - Cerro Gordo

Wp		Latitude	Longitude
1	36	58.6103	3 11.4059
2	36	58.6656	3 10.8335
3	36	59.1840	3 10.8647
4	36	59.2182	3 10.6349
5	36	59.5512	3 10.4435
6	37	00.7476	3 10.4580
7	37	00.4086	3 10.7124
8	37	00.8040	3 10.4784
9	37	01.7100	3 10.5504
10	37	01.7436	3 10.6242
11	37	01.7454	3 10.7166
12	37	01.4364	3 10.9902
13	37	00.8328	3 11.2494
14	37	00.2736	3 11.6970

35
Mecina-Bombarón - Acequia de los Castaños.

Wp		Latitude	Longitude
1	36	58.9056	3 09.4860
2	36	58.9752	3 09.5418
3	36	59.3460	3 09.3948
4	36	59.4192	3 09.3786
5	36	59.5158	3 09.3396
6	36	59.8764	3 09.3294
7	37	00.3336	3 09.1794
8	37	00.2292	3 09.1320
9	37	00.1842	3 08.9382
10	36	59.6676	3 09.2496

GLOSSARY OF SPANISH WORDS

a

abandonado	abandoned, in poor repair
abierto	open
acampamiento	camping
acantilado	cliff
acequia	water channel
agua	water
agua no potable	water (not drinkable)
agua potable	drinking water
alto	high
aparcamiento	parking
área recreativa	designated picnic spot; may have tables, water
arroyo	stream
autopista	main road, motorway
ayuntamiento	town hall

b

bajo	low
barranco	ravine
bocadillo	bread roll
bodegón	inn
bosque	wood

c

cabezo	peak, summit
cabra montés	mountain goat
calle	street
camino	trail, path, track
camino real	old donkey trail (lit. royal road)
camino cortado	road closed/blocked
carretera	main road
casa	house
casa rural	country house accommodation to let
cascada	waterfall
caserío	hamlet, village
cementario	cemetery
cerrado	closed
cerro	hill, mountain without a real peak
cerveza	beer
choza	shelter
clinica	clinic, hospital
colmena	bee hive
comida	food
cordillera	mountain range
correos	post office
cortijo	farmstead
costa	coast
coto privado de caza	private hunting area
Cruz Roja	Red Cross (medical aid)
cuesta	slope
cueva	cave
cumbre	summit

d

degollado	pass
derecha	right (direction)
desprendimiento	landslide

e

embalse	reservoir
ermita	chapel

f

farmacia	chemist
fiesta	holiday, celebration
finca	farm, country house
fuente	spring

g

gasolinera	petrol station
guagua	bus
Guardia Civil	police
guia	guide

h

hostal	hostel, accommodation
hoya	depression (geological)

i

iglesia	church
información	information
isla	island
izquierda	left (direction)

l

lago	lake
lavadero	laundry area (usually communal)
librería	bookshop
llano	plain
lluvioso	rainy
lomo	broad-backed ridge

m

mapa	map
mercado	market
mirador	lookout/viewing point
montaña	mountain

n

nublado	cloudy

o

oficina de turismo	tourist office

p

particular	private
peligroso	dangerous
pensión	guesthouse
pico	peak
pista	dirt road/track
pista forestal	forest road/track
playa	beach
plaza	square
policia	police
pozo	well
prohibido el paso	no entry
puente	bridge

puerto	port, mountain pass	*tapas*	bar snacks
		tienda	shop
r		*tinao*	typical Alpujarran
rambla	dry watercourse/riverbed		balcony/terrace
refugio	refuge, shelter	*tipico*	traditional bar/eating place
retama	broom-like shrub	*tormentoso*	stormy
rio	river, stream	*torre*	tower
robledal	oak woods	*torrente*	stream
roque	rock	*tuberia*	water pipe
ruta	route	**v**	
s		*valle*	valley
salida	exit	*vega*	meadow
senda	path, track	*ventoso*	windy
sendero	foot path	*vereda*	path, lane
sierra	mountain range	*vivero*	plant nursery, aboretum
sin salida	no through road/route	**z**	
t		*zona recreativa*	recreation area
tajo	cliff, escarpment		

APPENDICES

A PISTAS FORESTALES

The *pistas forestales* of the Alpujarras offer visitors an excellent opportunity to experience the high *sierras* at minimal effort. Drivers as well as trail and mountain bike riders are well served by this network of 'official' dirt roads which provide adventurous routes at altitude, well away from the tarmac. All the pistas were driveable and their routes accurately plotted during our research, but you should always take care on these off-raod routes. Take particular care in winter when routes may be snow-covered, and after/during wet weather.

Mountain bikers should not miss out on these *pistas forestales* which provide more than one hundred kilometres of off-road adventure, combining exertion with spectacular scenery. Note that, if ascending the **PF3**, there is a real danger of altitude sickness. If you start experiencing symptoms, stop and slowly descend.

Walk! The Alpujarras map sections show parts of the *pistas forestales* where these coincide with our walking routes. For full routes of **Pfs 1-5**, refer to the **Alpujarras Tour & Trail Super-Durable Map** (ISBN 1-904946-25-9 published by Discovery Walking Guides Ltd.). During our research we found a number of discrepancies between the *pistas forestales* as surveyed by ourselves, and the routes shown on other maps, including the official Spanish maps of the region.

PISTA FORESTAL 1 (PF1)
Lanjarón - Refugio Ventura (Access to Walk 10)

The definitive high mountain track. Worth driving even if you don't climb to **Caballo** as there are extraordinary views on the way up. N.B. Ignore the *Camino Cortado* signs above km 13.2. These are permanent fixtures 'just in case'!

- The track starts just before km 6 of the A348 at the western end of **Lanjarón**, opposite the park and next to the old bottling plant. Follow the signs for 'Tello'. The first stretch is concreted, but it soon gives way to dirt and very rough dirt at that. However, it's passable and the higher sections (above km 13.2) have been restabilised.

- km 6.6 **Fuente Pedro Calvo** (the **GR7** to **Niguelas** branches off just before the *fuente*). Reputed to have the best water in the Alpujarras (see photo on page 14).

- km 13.2 Turn left just above the third meteorological station.
- km 14.6 Pass a branch on the left descending to **Niguelas**.

- km 16.7 This is the last broad stretch before the track gets narrower and more 'impressive' - be prepared!

- km 17.5 There's a sign indicating a chain that no longer seems to be used.

- km 20.2 We pass a fourth meteorological station, shortly before the end of the dirt track.

PISTA FORESTAL 2 (PF2)
Ermita del Padre Eterno to **Puente Palo**, **El Robledal** & the **Río Lanjarón** below the **Lomas de Cáñar** & **Lanjarón**.

Good condition except for the last stretch which is a bit rocky. Access to Walks 13 & 14 and various strolls (see below).

- The track starts opposite the **Ermita del Padre Eterno**. 0.9 km east of the **Soportújar** turning off the **GR421**.

- At 500 metres it crosses the **GR7** (see Walk 2).

- km 2.4 A branch on the right leads to **O.Sel.Ling Bhuddist Centre** (5 km, visits between 3 and 6 p.m.) – see Walk 20.

- km 4.3 The tarmac ends and the dirt track starts at a Park Authority building soon after which we turn right at a sign for **Puente Palo**.

- km 10.8 The track crosses **Puente Palo**; there's a nice plunge pool above the bridge on the left bank of the **Río Chico** (200 metres before **Puente Palo** *Área Recreativa* - see Walk 11).

- km 11.2 The chained track on the right marks the start of Walk 13.

Strolls

(a) Take the dirt track climbing through the pine forest. Turn right on the first right-hand branch then right again at the **Acequia Grande** and follow the *acequia* back to the *Área Recreativa*. Also see Walk 13.

(b) 400 metres from western end of **Puente Palo** *Área Recreativa* (1.2 km from the **Cáñar** junction), several narrow goat paths climb to the right. Take the broadest, northernmost traces nearest the *Área Recreativa*. Climb through the woods, cross the field and turn right onto a dirt track. Leave the

---

dirt track as it bears left at the upper limit of the oak forest and follow the faint cow paths through the broom/furze. Cross the firebreak into the pine woods onto a minor track leading to the main dirt track (Walk 14) back down to the *Área Recreativa*.

(c) Start as per the last stroll, but turn left on the dirt track after the field and follow it down to the junction with the **Cáñar** branch; turn left to return to the start (1.2 km).

- km 13 Branch A descends on the left to **Cáñar** and the start of Walk 11. The track on the right climbs into **El Robledal**, the region's finest oak forest.

- km 13.8 **Casa Forestal de Cáñar**.

- km 15.2 Branch B descends on the left to **Lanjarón**.

- km 16.3 Branch C descends on the left to **Lanjarón**.

- km 18.9 Almost the end of the track and a convenient turning point. The main track bears right to climb to some *cortijos*, the narrower track ahead leads towards the bridge to the **Cortijo de Ballesteros**.

Stroll

(d) Take the narrower track upriver, cross the *cortijo* with goal posts in the garden, then cross the terraces to take a rough path descending to some nice bathing points beside the bridge to the **Cortijo Ballesteros**.

N.B.
Beware of improvising circuits via **Ballesteros** and the **Casa Forestal de Tello**; the **Tello** bridge is difficult to find if you don't already know it, it's a very steep climb back up from the lower part of the river, and it generally ends with having to scale a fence!

Climb back up from the river by the same path, but bear left away from the terraces to pass behind a large byre with a fenced corral, behind which you'll find a faint track leading to a clear dirt track back to the start

---

Branch A
Quite rough but passable. After descending 700 metres, a turning on the left leads to **Cortijo La Muda** (500 metres) currently being restored as a **Casa Rural** (see Fernando Vilchez – useful addresses)
km 3.8 The sharp bend just to the **East of Cerro Man** marks the starting point for Walk 11 (8.7 km from **Cáñar**)

Branch B
This is perhaps the most attractive descent with wonderful views of **Cáñar**.

Branch C
There's a couple of gates across this track, but they've always been open when we passed. The following distances are descending.

- km 0.6 A branch to the right leads down to the **Río Lanjarón**. The track crosses the **GR7** (Walk 1, Wp.7) & joins the **GR142** (Walk 9, Wp.10).

- km 12   The track/**GR142** joins the road at the eastern end of **Lanjarón** (Walk 1, Wp.1).

The 'Carretera de Veleta' to Hoya del Portillo (gr-411)

A well-maintained track, which will probably continue to be so since it's used by the Park Authority buses. Though it was never fully asphalted, this is still popularly called a *carretera* or 'road' in honour of its initial pretensions, and for some while it was celebrated as the highest road in Europe, crossing the Sierra Nevada from **Capileira** to **Güéjar-Sierra**. Nowadays though the higher stretches are closed to motorised traffic, thankfully, and the road is gradually being reclaimed for nature, both by her own efforts and those of ecologists. For cyclists and equestrians, the 50 km crossing to the ski station at **Pradollano** remains an attractive excursion, but it makes for pretty dull walking. This description ends at the **Hoya del Portillo** barrier.

Access to Walks 18, 19, 21 & 22, and four strolls (see below and Walk 22).

Set the odometer at zero at the sign for the coach-park 'P Autocares/Capileira' as you leave **Capileira**.

Stroll

(a) **Barranco de Cereza Robledal**: park in the large lay-by 700 metres after the coach-park.

N.B. The **Bubíon-Cebadilla** wayposted path crosses the road here. Go back down the road 100 metres and take the second dirt track on the left down to the junction with the GR7 (Walk 3, Wp.2). Bear left on the dirt track and stay on the dirt track when the GR7 bears right. Shortly before it ends, leave the dirt track on a clear path to the left marked by a small cairn. Follow the path up to the dirt track to **Pitres/Prado Toro** (see km 1.5 below). Bear left on the track then follow the road back to the car.

- km 1.5   Branch on the right signposted 'Cortijo Prado Toro' (see Appendix C, Sleeping), an alternative and more direct car-route to **Pitres**.

Strolls

(b) **Peña del Angel**. Not everybody's idea of a 'stroll' as the loop at the end involves some fairly athletic clambering about rocks. However, nobody's obliging you to climb, most of the route is on a dirt track, and almost equally breathtaking views can be had from just before the rocks. Follow the branch track to the Y-junction, then bear right and scramble up the rocky pinnacles of the **Peña** before descending at their southern end and following the dirt track back to the car.

(c) **Tajo de Soju**. Essentially a continuation of the last stroll, you could either combine the two or drive past the **Peña del Angel** and park at the junction with the **GR7** just after the two abandoned electricity towers. Continue on the dirt track till it ends in a little turning circle then take the path along the ridge and follow the firebreak till it starts to descend, a point that constitutes a natural *mirador* with some of the finest views to be had from anywhere of the **Poqueira Gorge** and the 3000 metre peaks. Especially recommended in winter.

- km 2.7 Branch on the left to **La Cebadilla** (Walk 18 & 19)

- km 3.8 On the right, **Pista Forestal 4** to **Trevélez**, signposted 'AR Río Bermejo 3km'

- km 5 End of asphalt, start of the dirt track

- km 7.1 Branch on the left to the start of Walk 21

- km 8.9 The firebreak on the left leads up to **Puerto Molina**, an alternative start to Walk 22 in spring if there's still snow below **Hoya del Portillo**.

- km 10.4 The barrier at **Hoya del Portillo** – so according to my odometer, it's not 13 km as the sign above **Capileira** claims!

PISTA FORESTAL 4 (PF4)
Capileira - Trevélez

A stony, dusty *pista forestal*, but well stabilised and easy to drive along in spring, summer and autumn. The nearer you get to **Trevélez**, the narrower and more dramatic it becomes, with magnificent views of the **Tahá**, **Loma de Juviles**, and **Peña de los Papos**. N.B. the 'GR' markings at the start are not 'GR' markings! (see Introduction, Waymarked Paths).

At km 3.8 of **Pista Forestal 3**, set the odometer at 0 and turn right at a sign saying 'Área Recreativa Río Bermejo 3 km'

- km 1 There's a nice picnic spot on a platform on the right amid small holm oak

- km 2.5 The bridge over the **Junta de los Ríos** (see Walk 23)

Strolls

(a) **Haza del Cerezo** (See Walk 23 Extension)

(b) **Barranco del Jabalí**
N.B. Path-finding maybe a problem.
Take the dirt track (N) on the western side of the bridge. Cross the **Río Chorrera** (also worth exploring for some fine bathing pools) and follow the goat tracks along the right bank of the **Jabalí**, climbing above a large chicane in the watercourse before descending to a makeshift dam forming a deep bathing pool. Cross the watercourse and follow the goat tracks south on the left bank of the **Jabalí** up to a dirt track above a goat farm. Take the dirt track back to **PF4** and the bridge.

- km 2.7 Branch on the left up to the goat farm mentioned in the last stroll.

- km 2.9 Turning on the right down to the *Área Recreativa*

Stroll

Wander through the *Área Recreativa* and descend to the bottom of the magnificent waterfall (see Walk 23).

- km 5.4 Branch on the right down to **Pórtugos**.

- km 11.1 Permanently water-logged section (passable at Easter and in summer).

- km 11.5 Section narrowed by landslip (again passable).

- km 16.7 Arrive just outside **Trevélez** on the main road into the **Barrios Medio & Alto**.

Juviles – Mecina-Bombarón

Highly recommended. A remote but well-stabilised track along most of which one can maintain a steady 30/40km an hour. None of our described walks start up here, but there is one stroll and also a route up to the **Peñon del Puerto** marked by cairns. Even if you don't walk though, the track of itself is attractive enough to justify an afternoon's exploration. After about 6km you start to get a real sense of high-mountain isolation.

If you're coming from the west, the track starts (on the left of the road) 2.6km after **Juviles**. Ignore the branch to the left immediately after you leave the road and, setting the odometer at 0, take the branch climbing on the right.

- km2.4 A branch on the right descends to **Bérchules**.

- km10.5 **Cortijo de Espino**

- km11.6 A branch on the left climbs towards the **Loma de Piedra Ventana**.

- km13 The **Río Chico**

- km17 The **Río Grande**

- km21.2 A branch on the right follows the firebreak described in Walk 34 down to join the **Mecina-Bombarón** branch (see below). Cairns on the left mark the ascent to **Peñon del Puerto**.

> **Stroll**
> Take the firebreak branch on the right and, after 100 metres join Walk 34 (Wps. 6-8).

- km23.8 The branch on the right is the main track down to **Mecina-Bombarón**.

Staying on the track north, we pass **Fuente de los Correllillos** (km24.6) shortly after which the track goes off our map. If you want to explore further, it's well worth visiting the tiny but exquisite little *Área Recreativa* at **Las Chorreras** (km28.2). After the **Río de Mecina** (km29.2), the landscape becomes more barren, but there's a nice track descending to the east of **Mecina-Bombarón** from km33.3.

If you're coming from the east, the branch emerging at km23.8, starts 1.8km from the western limits of **Mecina-Bombarón**, from where the following distances are relevant:

- km1.6 The track joins the **GR7** (Walk 7) and we turn left.

- km2.4 The **GR7** bears left on a minor track, we bear right.

- km5.6 We pass (on our left) the lower end of the firebreak-track from **Cerro Gordo** (see km21.2 above)

- km9.9 The track emerges at the km23.8 point mentioned above. Turn left for **Cerro Gordo**, 12.7km from the road.

B ADDITIONAL STROLLS

A few extras that didn't really fit in with any of the walks or *pistas forestales* but seemed too good to ignore!

The Río Chico above Bayacas
From **Bayacas** bridge follow the left bank of the **Río Chico** (N). Pass under the main road bridge and climb to the left of the silt-dam for a pleasant picnic spot and some small plunge pools. If you're feeling more adventurous and energetic, continue up the right bank along rough goat trails littered with fallen trees to a high waterfall and a wilder glade. If you really want to get the blood moving, cross the glade to join a broader path winding up to a junction. Carry straight on for a vertiginous *acequia* path to source, or turn right for a threshing circle with fine views south over the valley and the **Sierra Lújar** and, north, up to **Puente Palo** and the **Loma de Cáñar**.

The Mirador de Poqueira
Hundreds of people stop here everyday, but few realise the views from the little watchtower along the ridge are even more dramatic. To be honest, few even notice the watchtower! 400 metres after the **Pampaneira** Fina station (in the direction of **Pitres**) take the rough path from the *mirador* along the ridge to the outcrop of rocks for giddying views of the gorge.

The Acequia de Cuna
A stroll that's also a paddle - providing there's water in the *acequia*; if there isn't the fun is dramatically diminished. We often walk alongside *acequias*, here we walk in one. Take your plastic sandals. 10 metres south of the km23 sign on the **Trevélez-Busquístar** road, directly opposite the metal sign for the **Trevélez** campsite, a tiny path between two young plane trees climbs very steeply about 15 metres to the *acequia*. For an easier access, take the path 75 metres further south where the road bears right. Follow the *acequia* south to the second large outcrop of rock, beyond which it has been abandoned, becoming increasingly overgrown, eventually petering out after a fence in the **Barranco de la Bina**. Return the same way, taking the alternative access path for an easier descent.

The best swimming pool in the Alpujarras
Two kilometres from the **Trevélez** bridge (in the direction of **Juviles**), park in the lay-by just after the **Barranco de los Castaños**. Take the path below the crash barriers before the next bend to descend to the river. At the Y-junction, bear left for a pleasant picnic/bathing spot under immense poplars, right for a deep swimming pool below the metal footbridge. **N.B.** Don't swim too near the waterfall on the off-chance that some debris might be pitched over.

Telephone numbers below are shown in red, fax numbers in blue and web addresses/email addresses in green. To dial phone/fax numbers from outside Spain add 00 34 first.

PHONE NUMBERS, WEB ADDRESSES, RECOMMENDATIONS
Though all reasonable care has been taken to ensure the following information is up-to-date, experience suggests the authorities in Spain change their phone lines with alarming regularity.

RESERVATIONS

www.turandalucia.com   www.turgranada.com
www.rusticblue.com   www.hotelandalucia.com
www.associacion.org   www.lanjaron.org
www.spainyoga.com/PropertyRentals.htm
www.descubrealpujarra.com

Early morning bus Capileira - Mirador de Trevélez
To book a seat on the early morning bus from **Capileira** to the **Mirador de Trevélez** (see Walk 22) 686 414 576.

See below for hotels with websites

SLEEPING, EATING AND DRINKING

(RG) = Rough Guide recommendations

Lanjarón
(RG) Hotel España   958 770 187   958 770 187
(RG) Apartamentos Castillo Aladima
                          www.alcadima.com   958 770 809
(RG) Bar/Hostal Galvez   958 770 702
(RG) Restaurante Manolete, Calle Queipo de Llano
Hotel Nuevo Manolete, Calle San Sebastián
                          www.lanjaron.org   958 770 773

Órgiva
Hotel Taray   958 784 525
                          www.paginas-amarillas.es/on/line/htaray
(RG) Hostal/Restaurante Alma Alpurrajeña   958 784 085
(RG) Hostal Mirasol   958 785 159
(RG) Bar/Restaurante El Semáforo

Cáñar
Fernando Vilchez 696 89 47 99. Has a fine apartment to rent in **Cáñar** (€36 a day) and is currently restoring **Cortijo La Muda**, near **Puente Palo**, where he'll rent rooms (ideally placed for a three day excursion from **Cáñar** to **Pico Alegas**). No English, but he does speak perfect French. He's also an agent for guided walks and paragliding and is willing to act as a landrover taxi.

María Domínguez Pérez / José Alvarez Guerrero 958 785 306 / 958 784

444 / 630 482 371. They hold one of the local bars and have houses to rent near **Puente Palo**.

Soportújar
(RG) Bar/Hostal Correillo, Calle Real		958 787 578
Mirador de Boabdil	958 784 965	958 785 055

Carataunas
(RG) El Montañero	www.hotelmontanero.com	958 787 528

Pampaneira
Hostal/Bar/Restaurante Guillerm.	958 763 023

A must for carnivores. The black pudding is extraordinary. (See Walk 2)

Hostal/Restaurante Casa Diego,	
Plaza de la Libertad	958 763 102
Hostal Ruta del Mulhacén	958 763 010
Pensión/Restaurante Pampaneira	958 763 002

Bubíon
(RG) Pensión/Apartamentos Las Terrazas		958 763 034
Villa Turística	www.villabubion.com	958 763 909
(RG) Restaurante La Artesa, Calle Carretera		

Capileira
(RG) Méson/Hostal Poqueira	958 763 048	958 763 048
Fonda/Restaurante El Tilo		958 763 048
Finca Los Llanos	958 763 206	958 763 071
Poqueira Refuge		958 343 349
Apartamentos Vista Veleta		958 763 070

La Tahá
Pitres: Hotel San Roque		958 857 528
Refugio de los Albergues		958 766 004
Apartamentos Posada La Tahá		958 343 041
Cortijo Prado Toro	www.pradotoro.com	958 343 240
Pórtugos: Hostal Mirador		958 766 014
Busquístar:		
Hostal Mirador de la Alpujarra	958 857 470	958 857 470
Casa Sonia	958 857 528	958 857 528
	sonia@teleline.es	
Ferreirola: Sierra y Mar	www.sierraymar.com	958 766 171
Mecina:		
Hotel Albergue de Mecina	958 766 255	958 766 254
	www.hotelalberguedemecina.com	

Trevélez
Alcazaba de Busquístar	www.alpujarralcazaba.com	
		958 858 687
(RG) Hotel La Fragua	958 858 614	958 858 626
		/958 858 573
Pensíon Regina		958 858 564

Cástaras

Pensíon Maria   958 855 547

Juviles
(RG) Fonda/Restaurante Bar Fernandez   958 769 030
Pensíon Tino   958 769 174

Bérchules
El Halcón   958 768 733
Hotel los Bérchules   958 769 00   958 852 530
                             hot.berchules@interbook.net
(RG) La Posada   958 852 541   958 852 541
(RG) Fonda/Restaurante Carayol   958 769 092

Cádiar
Apartamentos Sitio de Estar El Cadi   958 850 469
Apartamentos Ruta de la Alpujarra   958 768 059
Hostal Alquería de Morayma   www.alqueriamorayma.com
                                                   958 343 221
(RG) Hostal Montoro   958 768 068

Mecina-Bombarón
Apartamentos Mirador de Avellano   958 131 498
Los Molinos   www.arrakis.es/-molinos   858 851 076
Casas Blancas   www.casasblancas.es.vg   58 851 151
                             www.casasblancas.turincon.com

Bayacas
El Bancal   958 784 595/958 785 579

Campsites
Capileira   958 763 419
Órgiva   958 784 307
                             www.perso.wanadoo.es/campingorgiva
Puerta de la Alpujarra   958 784 450
                             www.campings.net/puertadelalpujarra
Pitres   958 766 111   958 766 111
Trevélez   958 858 735   958 858 735
                  www.teleline.es/personal/cam-trev/camping.htm

Supermarkets
Supermarkets are small and varied; some are awful, some very good. The best
we found are La Depensa next to the tobacconist in **Órgiva**, and El Molino,
Busquístar. The Komo-Komo in **Bubío**n, Spar and Coviran in **Trevélez** and
Supermercado in **Alcútar** are OK, too. For cheap bulk purchases try Dia in
Órgiva.

BUSES & TAXIS

Alsina Graells,   www.alsinagraells.es   958 185 480
the main bus company

La Tahá Bus, the local company   950 510 800

Getting a taxi can be a challenge. If the harvest needs bringing in, something more lucrative turns up, or the driver's simply busy in a bar, service may be suspended. At the same time, restaurant owners and complete strangers have been known to offer lifts to stranded tourists, and hitching is always an option.

Juan Funes   958 785 331/619 957 817. Local & landrover taxi based in **Órgiva**. No English, but says he can be contacted through his English speaking friend Eladio at the Hotel Taray (958 784 525). By Alpujarran standards a model of reliability, though sometimes absent in Granada.

The best way of finding transport is to ask on the spot. That said, other taxi numbers you might try, are as follows:

Bérchules	958 753 061 & 958 764 047
Bubíon	958 763 148
Busquístar	958 766 036
Cadíar	958 750 029 & 958 750 051 & 958 750 064
Capileira	958 763 125
Cástaras	958 753 035
Lanjarón	958 770 057 & 958 770 097 & 958 770 000 & 958 770 160
Órgiva	958 785 190 & 958 785 417 & 958 785 131 & 958 785 225
Pampaneira	958 763 002
Pitres	958 766 005
Pórtugos	958 766 006
Trevélez	958 858 546 & 958 858 537

MISCELLANEOUS INFORMATION

Nevedensis   www.nevednesis.com   958 763 127
- local information about the Alpujarras

Tourist Offices
Lanjarón   958 770 282
Pampaneira   958 763 301

Turismo Alpujarra   958 784 495   958 784 484
c/Lora Ramayo 17/18400 Órgiva   alta-alpujarra@asociacion-tierra.org

National Meteorological Institute   906 365 365
Local long-range forecasts are posted outside the Nevedensis office in Pampaneira.

Emergencies
Emergency co-ordination centre Andalucía   112
Emergency Civil Guard   062
Red Cross   913 354 545
Casa de Socorro   958 770 002
(local medical emergencies)

Sierra Nevada Administrative Centre
                                     958 026 310   958 026 300
National Park Visitors' Centres
(weekends)   958 340 625 / 958 763 127
Spain's national parks website   www.mma.es/parques

A pamphlet of local addresses, telephone numbers and festival dates for the

Alpujarras is available from:
Tursimo Andaluz SA   952 836 369   952 838 785
Centro Internacional de Turismo de Andalucia
Crta. Nac. 340 – Cádiz-Málaga km 189.6
29600 Marbella.

For detailed information/updates about the GR142 - Paco   958 784 340

… about the GR7 - Jesus Espinosa   659 109 662
(if you can't get through, contact him at the Nevedensis office)

Lanjarón Spa (balneario):   958 771 070   958 770 137
                                   www.aguadelanjaron.es

Horse-riding from Trevélez
Rutas a Caballo   958 858 601

For a small but carefully chosen selection of books in English, try Atenea on Calle Lora Tamayo (behind the bus stop) in **Órgiva**.

Walk! Wire-O Spiral Bound Guidebooks are designed to be used with:

- DWG's plastic slipcover (PSC), which prevents the binding from catching on pockets and increases durability -
- - and our clear plastic All Weather Book Bag (AWBB) with grip-top seal which allows the book to be folded back displaying 2 pages, then sealed, impervious to weather conditions.

To obtain your PSC and AWBB for this book, send a C5 (9 x 7 inch) SAE with 47p stamp, to:
(Code 9781904946232)
Discovery Walking Guides
10 Tennyson Close
Northampton NN5 7HJ